NAKED

Black Women Bare All About Their
Skin, Hair, Hips, Lips, and Other Parts

Edited by Ayana Byrd and Akiba Solomon

Foreword by Sonia Sanchez

A PERIGEE BOOK

THE BERKLEY PUBLISHING GROUP
Published by the Penguin Group
Penguin Group (USA) Inc.
375 Hudson Street, New York, New York 10014, USA
Penguin Group (Canada), 10 Alcorn Avenue, Toronto, Ontario M4V 3B2, Canada
(a division of Pearson Penguin Canada Inc.)
Penguin Books Ltd., 80 Strand, London WC2R 0RL, England
Penguin Group Ireland, 25 St. Stephen's Green, Dublin 2, Ireland (a division of Penguin Books Ltd.)
Penguin Group (Australia), 250 Camberwell Road, Camberwell, Victoria 3124, Australia
(a division of Pearson Australia Group Pty. Ltd.)
Penguin Books India Pvt. Ltd., 11 Community Centre, Panchsheel Park, New Delhi—110 017, India
Penguin Group (NZ), cnr. Airborne and Rosedale Roads, Albany, Auckland 1310, New Zealand
(a division of Pearson New Zealand Ltd.)
Penguin Books (South Africa) (Pty.) Ltd., 24 Sturdee Avenue, Rosebank, Johannesburg 2196, South Africa
Penguin Books Ltd., Registered Offices: 80 Strand, London WC2R 0RL, England

Copyright © 2005 by Ayana Byrd and Akiba Solomon
Individual authors hold the copyright for their own essay
Cover design by Ben Gibson
Cover photo by G. Giraldo

PRINTING HISTORY
Perigee trade paperback edition / August 2005

PERIGEE is a registered trademark of Penguin Group (USA) Inc.
The "P" design is a trademark belonging to Penguin Group (USA) Inc.

Library of Congress Cataloging-in-Publication Information

Naked : black women bare all about their skin, hair, hips, lips, and other parts / edited by Ayana Byrd and Akiba Solomon ; foreword by Sonia Sanchez.
    p. cm.
    Includes index.
    ISBN 0-399-53163-7
    1. African American women—Psychology. 2. African Americans—Race identity. 3. Body image—United States. 4. Beauty, Personal—United States. 5. African American women—Biography. I. Byrd, Ayana D. II. Solomon, Akiba.

E185.86.N34 2005
305.48'8'896073—dc22

2004060136

PRINTED IN THE UNITED STATES OF AMERICA

10   9   8   7   6   5   4   3   2   1

DEDICATION

We dedicate this work to our mothers, Rochelle Nichols-Solomon and Stephanie Williams; our grandmothers, Mamie Nichols and Carolyn Solomon, Florence Price and Geraldine Byrd; and to our godmothers, Rosemary Matthews and Karen Winston.

ACKNOWLEDGMENTS

We would like to thank our families for their moral support; our contributors for giving their all; G. Giraldo for the beautiful portraits; Joicelyn Dingle for her tireless celeb-wrangling; Sonia Sanchez for her powerful words; Marie Brown for structure and encouragement; and our editor, Dara Stewart, for her unshakable belief in *Naked*.

We'd also like to thank Karen Addison, Jessica Chong, Santana Dempsey, Angeliq Turner, Raphael Romana, Shani Parrish, Mimi Valdés, Karen R. Good, Margeaux Watson, Jevon Johnson, Willie Nattiel, Christian Bernard, Zurn Porter, Karla Radford, Shyne, Hilary Beard, Francesco Samichelli, Carole Hall, Julia Chance, Daniella Cobb, Alexis Bell, Jermaine Hall, Datwon Thomas, Kofi Taha, Ahmir Thompson, Margaret Prescod-Cisse, Shaun Gee, Jessica Cohen, Marsha and Len Burnett, Yvette Schure, Tracie Miller, Hillary Weston, Karen Taylor-Bass, Tim Murphy,

Acknowledgments

Michele Pierce, Lil' Mo, Louise Sloan, Jeannie Kim, Charles Bjorklund, Jordan Barnes, and Tanya McKinnon.

Finally, we must acknowledge some of the activists, artists, athletes, models, and writers who built the foundation for *Naked*: Debbie Allen, Maya Angelou, India.Arie, Erykah Badu, Sartje Baartman, Lisa Bonet, Gwendolyn Brooks, Elizabeth Catlett, Kathleen Cleaver, Cathy Cohen, Lucille Clifton, Edwidge Danticat, Julie Dash, Angela Davis, Althea Gibson, Nikki Giovanni, Eloise Greenfield, Pam Grier, Whoopi Goldberg, Lauryn Hill, bell hooks, Hilda Hutcherson, Iman, Judith Jamison, Lisa Jones, Marion Jones, June Jordan, Florence Griffith-Joyner, Jayne Kennedy, Nella Larsen, Queen Latifah, MC Lyte, Audre Lorde, Annie Tunrbo Malone, Kierna Mayo, Joan Morgan, Jessica Care Moore, Toni Morrison, Nehanda Obiyodun, Suzan Lori Parks, Beah Richards, Faith Ringgold, Fatima Robinson, Tricia Rose, Salt-N-Pepa, Danzy Senna, Assata Shakur, Ntozake Shange, Nina Simone, Lorna Simpson, Yvette Smalls, Stephanie Stokes Oliver, Harriet Beecher Stowe, Susan L. Taylor, Sojourner Truth, Cicely Tyson, Linda Villarosa, Alice Walker, Rebecca Walker, Madame CJ Walker, Rebecca Walker, Michelle Wallace, Faye Wattleton, Carrie Mae Weems, Alek Wek, Serena and Venus Williams, Debra Willis, Oprah Winfrey, and Gail Elizabeth Wyatt.

CONTENTS

Contents

Contents

FOREWORD

One night in 1984 I was leaving City Hall, coming from a late meeting in the mayor's office. As I came outside, a man, a White man, drove up and yelled out to me, "You want some of this?" And as I looked towards him and his car I saw that he had his pants open and he was shaking his penis at me.

I had thought that with my coat and my purse and my briefcase, I would be seen that night as a professional, as the professor of English at Temple University that I was. But all he saw was a Black woman outdoors at night. He saw a prostitute. A streetwalker. An easy, available Black woman. He didn't see me.

It's always a shocker when you see yourself one way, but many people in the world view you very differently. I dealt with this particular shock by writing a poem that made a few people say, "Sonia, I just don't understand why you write these really wicked poems." I told them, "Because there are some really wicked mothers out here, and they need to be identified as such." There's no nice language for that.

In this country, from the very beginning, the slave masters put these Black, often naked, women on auction blocks. What these White men saw was free access—a wildness, an exoticness in this very prudish society that was developing.

In *Incidents in the Life of a Slave Girl*, Linda Brent recalled how at age eleven or twelve, the men began to whisper vulgar things in her ear, preparing her for her eventual rape. So they wanted to begin the process of familiarizing her with the language of sex, the language that removed her from becoming a decent young girl.

Some enslaved women would be forced to sleep at the foot of the bed so that it would be convenient for the master to take his pleasure. When masters saw us, they saw rape, they saw possession. They saw ownership. They saw beauty. They saw vulnerability. They saw women uncovered and unprotected. There were no Victorian women here.

So the bodies of Black women have written a history and a herstory in America. A herstory that has placed Black women not just as enslaved women who hated slavery, but as women who supposedly enjoyed the rape and pillage by their slave masters. We can't change the past, so our words become our best defense against its legacy.

One of the things that we did as African women in the 1960s was to put ourselves on the world stage. We demanded to be taken seriously and insisted that people see us as human beings who had something to say, who weren't just there to satiate sick sexual urges or to fulfill domestic demands.

We'd say simple things like, "I am a beautiful Black woman." That meant many things. It meant, "I like my body, if it's big or small. I like my face, whether I'm a raving beauty or not. I like my nose, whether it's narrow or flat, flat, flat. I like my big lips. I like my eyes. I like my hair." Since some women then did not like their full lips or their nappy hair, or their wide noses or even their Blackness, this affirmation of love for self and body was a revolutionary action.

And yet today, women are still looked at as body, not as mind. And many Black women still don't consider ourselves beautiful. We're so inundated with certain kinds of beauty on the television and in the world, with certain hair, and bodies that have to be a certain color, and that are thin, thin, thin *and* curvy, curvy, curvy in all of the "right" places.

Many of us know that we are smart, but we do not believe that we are beautiful. But if we are going to go out and change this world, we cannot be crippled on that level. We must go out whole, knowing that we are beautiful and Black; that we carry all African women with us; and that we are able to defend ourselves against anyone who regards us as prostitutes and whores and who try to convince us that we are who they think we are.

Every one of us has to look in a mirror and see herself as beautiful before other people will. You can't rely on a man or woman to tell you, because if he or she disappears you're lost again. You have to see your beauty behind your eyes. You must make it real with words. You must say, "This is who I am forever, and I am indeed beautiful and smart."

As a girl, I was like everybody else. I looked at my breasts; they were small and I didn't like them. I looked at my hair and it was curly, curly, curly, and I didn't like it because it wasn't straight like my sister's. I didn't expect the things that pretty girls got. This lasted until I was a young woman, when I decided that I was beautiful and smart.

One day after my graduation from Hunter College, I was on the Number 2 train going home to Harlem. I missed my stop and wound up having to get off at 135th Street and Lenox Avenue. Above ground, I passed this building I'd never seen. It was the Schomburg Library. I went inside and asked Ms. Jeanne Hudson, "What kind of library is this?" She said it was a library that had books only by and about Black folks. I said, with my smart nineteen-and-half-year-old self, "There must not be many books in here." She smiled, sat me down and brought me three books: *Souls of Black Folk*, *Their Eyes Were Watching God*, and *Up From Slavery*.

I began to read *Their Eyes Were Watching God* and soon there were tears in my eyes. I had never seen a Black woman like Janie in literature, never seen this beautiful kind of writing, never seen anything like this. That day in the Schomburg, I found me in words, I found my pain, my beauty, my possibilities. I found love, a sense of home.

So when I became a poet, I wanted to use my words to help others see themselves the way *Their Eyes Were Watching God* helped me see myself.

One day I went to a school and read some of my poetry for elementary students. The poem ended, "pretty like you and you and you and you." There was this little sister sitting there, and she said, "I'm not pretty." I said, "Stand up, walk with me." We walked around the gym. I said, "I'm pretty like you're pretty. You've got pretty lips, pretty hair, pretty eyes." She's looking at me from afar, not really believing it. A few days later I wrote a little ballad for her and delivered it to her at the school. She was a child who had been made tough already. But when I gave her the poem she smiled and some of the toughness melted away.

None of us can deliver healing words to every school or home in the world, though. And it'll take more than one poet or storyteller to counteract the madness girls' and women's bodies are subjected to.

Naked does its part. It provides for the mind, for women who still think that beauty means something fixed or prescribed. *Naked* provides the mind with the messages for change. To read the words of older and younger women about how they've learned to look in the mirror without turning away is empowering. The different stories show what beauty really is.

One of the questions posed in the essays and oral memoirs is, "Who are these bodies for?" These bodies are for ourselves. There should be a conversation that we have with them: "It's heavy. That's OK, I like it." "It's thin, that's OK, I like it." "It's short, that's OK, I like it." "This is who I am, this is mine. It will be with me until I take my last breath. So I like and love it and will protect it against any invasion."

Because when you talk about beauty, you're really talking about what it means to be human. When you find the core of humanity inside yourself, that's when you know that you are beautiful.

We are beautiful because we are coming at ourselves from the inside, as activists. The moment we move and do things on this earth, the moment we truly understand our herstory, we become expressions of beauty.

I'm not saying that people won't say things that make your head pop back sometimes, but you can always go into yourself. You can ask your body, "Okay, cover up that wound for me, if you don't mind. Beautify that place there that someone has hurt." And then you go out again and you're okay. You say, "Good morning world, how you be? I'm the real deal" and you smile at yourself.

Sonia Sanchez
Philadelphia, Pennsylvania

(To my sister, Anita Patricia Meca, and my children,
who make me feel beautiful.)

INTRODUCTION

lack women have come a long way since Sojourner Truth opened fire on America's Victorian White–pedestal definition of womanhood with her infamous 1851 "Ain't I a Woman?" speech. We are no longer inspected and peddled on auction blocks, raped willy-nilly by our deed-holders, legally forbidden to read or teach, or forced to bear babies to be sold down some river. We are not chattel. Whether we're standing at billion-dollar podiums or crawling in $5.00 crack dens, no one denies our womanhood.

Now, our humanity is a whole different story. Black women's parts—particularly our butts, hips, thighs, breasts, lips, skin, and hair—are continually overemphasized, fetishized, derided, "improved," trend-spotted, and otherwise objectified. These parts are the subject of constant critique and appraisal by male and female passersby of all creeds, by popular media, and, once we've undergone the inevitable process of internalization, by ourselves. Year by year, parts of the bodies we're born with are declared "in" or "out," too thin or thick, too flat or round, too straight or nappy, too light or dark. And while Black women's bodies get all the play, our thoughts and feelings go unarticulated or flat-out ignored.

So maybe we shouldn't have been surprised by the vacant stares we received when we told some of our male and female friends, colleagues, and family members that we were editing a book about Black women's body images. A few stumbled on the words "body image"—they'd never heard the term that describes how a person's perception of their physical form impacts their overall self-image and behavior. Others informed us that unless we were producing a Debra Willis–style coffee table book of Black nudes, the title, *Naked*, was a form of false advertising. And then there were the folks who intimated that discussing body image was strictly a "pastime" of college students, career academics, and White feminists.

Instead of debating semantics, we adjusted our description of the project. "An anthology of personal essays and oral memoirs about Black women's body images" turned into "Black women are gonna talk and write about how they feel about their bodies and how these feelings affect their self-esteem and behavior."

Naked is about what a dark-skinned teenager sees in the mirror after a decade of watching music videos. It's about the twentysomething who once believed that the only pitfall of binge eating was her inability to wear size 6s and date fine men. It's about the woman in her early thirties who overidentified with the 1980s stereotype of the big, brown, poor "Welfare Queen." It's about the sixty-eight-year-old grandmother who altered her physical self to become her version of a pinup girl, beauty queen, revolutionary, and ultimately the proverbial Black Earth mother.

While stories like these are the marrow of *Naked*, they weren't the impetus. In 2001, Ayana decided to edit a contemporary collection of personal essays and oral memoirs after she realized that men's demeaning catcalls made her feel so ashamed of her breasts that she'd taken to wearing hoodies in 95-degree weather. Akiba accepted her invitation to co-edit the book after relinquishing her position at a major hip-hop magazine, where she spent too much energy explaining why it wasn't okay to use an unidentified Black woman's naked butt cheeks as a prop in a photo shoot.

While brushes with sexism spurred both of us, we did not create *Naked* to shout out the problematic behavior that some men exhibit. This book is bigger than the dark-skinned passerby who calmly informed Akiba that she was an "ugly *black* bitch with no butt" after she failed to respond to his lustful once-over. It is more than the White men in her adopted city, Barcelona, Spain, who whisper "how much?" in Ayana's ear because they have decided that the combination of Black skin and a vagina equals sex-for-sale. No, *Naked* is about more than reaction. Its purpose is to create a dignified, safe, comfortable, intraracial space for Black women to discuss our bodies and define ourselves.

After all, if anyone needs to be battling body demons on a conscious, constructive level, it is us. By 2004, Black women were the fastest rising group of women being diagnosed with eating disorders. Many of us are dangerously overweight, and unprecedented numbers are turning to elective cosmetic surgery to "fix" what we consider unsightly. The majority of us chemically straighten our hair, spending $12 billion annually to transform the structure of our tresses out of "necessity" rather than choice.

What's more, Black conventional wisdom demands that we openly accept and celebrate our bodies. "Strong Black Women," we are taught, are a monolith of pear-shaped, curvy, sashaying, devil-may-care neck-rollers. Countless body satisfaction studies use White women as the control group, consequently focusing on weight and ignoring skin tone and hair texture. The skewed result is that Black women seem more self-assured, lending clinical credence to our unwritten cultural rules. Perhaps the stereotype of the innately confident Black woman would be positive if it were true. But we are human. Whether we admit it or not, we, too, internalize unattainable beauty standards and hold warped notions of the purpose of our bodies.

It's no secret that the most common way to talk about the female body in America is to discuss how it should be fixed and how much it appeals to men. From "reality" shows peddling makeovers to front-porch conversations about where to get the tightest weave, the message is obvious: what we're born with is not going to get us very far.

Movies, music, women's magazines, news broadcasts, popular fiction, commercials, sporting events, and retail racks are major purveyors of this message. It often turns girls into women who view their shape, complexion, hair texture, and sexuality with varying degrees of trepidation, discomfort, ambivalence, and ignorance.

Naked is one alternative to these market-driven messages. Through the words of everyday women, professional writers, and celebrities who provide our public face, *Naked* explores the complex influences of our families, friends, institutions, and the ever-present elephants in the room: White supremacy and patriarchy.

But for all that it is, *Naked* is not a book of "isms." Although individual pieces address racism, sexism, or capitalism, it is a collection of personal stories. Because this book emphasizes emotions rather than intellect, some of these stories may seem contradictory, unresolved, and even tragic. We also acknowledge that the collection is overwhelmingly urban, Northeastern, middle class, and heterosexual, a consequence of proximity and limited resources. However, we feel that many experiences in this book cut across particular circumstance—that empowerment lies in self-definition and shared experience.

And we joyfully admit that we are not reinventing the wheel. Thank God Black writers, artists, performers, thinkers, entrepreneurs, activists, athletes and models have laid the foundation for *Naked!* (Please read every single name on our acknowledgments page.)

All told, *Naked* is an entry point, a way to get mothers talking to daughters, women talking to men, and, most significant, women talking to themselves about how to form our identities, claim our ideals, and come to terms with the relationship we have with our bodies. Nothing less than our humanity is at stake.

SOWING BEAUTY

Bethann Hardison

As told to Ayana Byrd and Akiba Solomon

Photo by: Torkil Gudnason.

D o you know how many magazines you can buy and throw out, not even getting a chance to read them all? Everything today is so media-driven. Everyone finds a way to make a business, so everyone becomes an image, a style, a look.

This is so different from how it was. Things were simpler when I came up as a young woman in the '60s and '70s. We didn't have as much, but there were more artistic spirits. We were still discovering and creating things. Anybody could be somebody. There was no prescribed way that you had to look to be a success in the bohemian circles in which I traveled.

I'd grown up listening to my parent's stories about their days in the '40s as well-known jitterbug dancers, when folks would bar them from places like the Cotton Club and the High Brown Babies ball because their hair didn't glide through a small-tooth comb and their skin was darker than a paper bag. That's what was so genius about the world of runway modeling when I started out. People didn't select you because of what you looked like. You could be Black, White, light skinned, brown skinned, or dark skinned with a full mouth and large eyes like mine.

Style was what was important. Style is something that "is," it's not a "like." It's just in your bones. It moves gently like the sea does, not fast like a trend. And I had it, that's how I was successful. When I was on the runway, I was a stick figure, but I'd wear the clothes and dance and draw the crowd, and I was this big sensation.

Now that I'm older, I'm too busy being worried about the spirit of my body to get caught up in its physicality. When you reach a certain age, things really change. So there are things I don't like, ways I could eat better. But at the end of the day, it's simply something to be maintained; a vehicle to get me from here to there.

When I think about young people today, though, it seems so hard. Everything around them shows how good you are supposed to look. The body doesn't seem to be strong enough because the mind is so manipulated and challenged from outside influences. The spirit has to fight to even exist. That's why we have to plant the seeds early.

With my granddaughter, Sophia, I know what she sees around her. Most of the kids in her school are White. When she turns on the TV, the women in the videos are light-skinned. Her mother is also fair, but Sophia is closer to my complexion. And last year, when she was just six years old, she started to have issues about her skin. Now she's looking at her hair, wishing it was longer. But I don't freak out. Hair extensions aren't going to make her feel better about herself. Instead I keep telling her so matter-of-factly that her hair looks beautiful, that she is beautiful. I just keep on planting the seeds.

Along with supermodel Iman, **Bethann Hardison** co-founded the Black Girls Coalition, an organization that pushed for greater inclusion of Black models. The former runway model heads up Bethann Management, a talent agency.

PIROPOS

Ayana Byrd

Photo by G. Giraldo.

"I bet your pussy stinks, too!"

It wasn't a furious lover, a rival, or an inappropriate gynecologist yelling insults at me down a crowded midtown Manhattan street. It was a strange man, a Black man, who was acting out because he hadn't gotten his way.

And it was at this moment that I, a lifelong pacifist who could still locate my peace sign earrings from middle school, knew I had it in me to shoot a man.

This was in 1996, fifteen years after I prematurely developed breasts and learned that my body had become an object for men to appraise and comment upon. And a decade-and-a-half of never feeling full ownership over myself had culminated in seething rage in front of Radio City Music Hall on this hot July day.

NAKED

I was standing at the corner, waiting for the light to change. I'd just noticed that everyone around me was White, dressed in professional attire, and looked older—like real adults. I am Black, was wearing a spaghetti-strap tank top and an ankle-skimming flowing skirt that said "cute" more than "corporate," and was twenty-three—that age when only the IRS and student loan agencies take you for a grown-up. As I wondered if I appeared out of place to anyone else, a Black man, fortysomething, in cargo pants, and sane-looking at first glance, came way too close. He was looking hungrily in the direction of my chest; I jumped. Then I tried to ease unnoticed to the opposite crowd gathered at the corner.

That, apparently, was my big mistake.

"That's what's wrong with all you Black bitches. Why none of y'all can get a man!" he screamed, leaning out in front of the row of shocked people who stood between us. "Damn, woman, I was just trying to get a taste of titty."

At that moment the light changed and I crossed the street, mortified and a little scared that I'd managed to infuriate a crazy person. When there was about a half block of distance between us I slowed down. And then . . .

"I bet your *pussy* stinks, too!"

He was so loud that I had no problem hearing him over the taxis, the tourists, and even a construction site. Especially the way he spat out "pussy," like mine was the nastiest, dirtiest one he'd ever been forced to consider.

I must have looked as freaked out as I felt, because another man, a suited White man, had had enough. "Why don't you leave her alone? What's wrong with you?" he demanded in the way that people who are used to being obeyed are so good at. "What do you want? Go on, walk away!"

Mumbling "Thank you" for the unexpected assist, I turned before I was supposed to and walked the long way back to the publishing office where I worked.

I'd escaped the lunatic but not the effects of his verbal taunting. I internalized it all, and felt unnerved but mostly embarrassed. Even a little betrayed by my own titties for offering something so tantalizing that it had sparked a scene.

That wasn't the last time I blamed myself for on-the-street ignorance. Now, to ask anyone who knows me, they would call the previous sentence an outright lie, saying that I am ruthless and bold in my withering looks and icy put-downs to men and boys who take it upon themselves to hiss, catcall, and speak their minds as I pass.

But it's a cover-up, a lie, my attempt to deflect from the discomfort that their stares and words generate. Observe how I am always fidgeting, shifting my weight from one foot to the other, never knowing what to do with my arms as I stand listening to a story or having small talk at a party. I don't feel completely at home in my own skin.

A stranger might assume that the uneasiness stems from an extended awkward phase filled with pimples and excess body fat. But no, I've never fought to lose that last five pounds and acne was never more than an occasional annoyance. Quite the opposite, I was generally thought of as one of the "pretty girls," by both family and friends. My skin may have been one or two shades too brown to be considered desirable in the color-obsessed

1980s, but my long, soft-textured hair seemed to overcompensate. And my body, all 5′2″ and 104 pounds of it, always struck a popular balance with its C-cup chest and round, quintessentially.

If confidence were only dependent on other's opinions, I'd be fine. If confidence were only dependent on thinking you looked okay each morning as you stood in the mirror naked, I'd still be all right. But my confidence falters when I wrestle with what this body is for, who it is meant to please, and how I am supposed to navigate it through spaces both social and sexual.

My childhood, just like everyone else's, provides all the necessary clues as to how I got screwed up. On the good side, neither of my parents acted like bodies were something shameful. Before we had air-conditioning and had to brave humid Philadelphia summers, each walked around the house in their underwear. If I came into a room and they hadn't finished getting dressed, no one jumped or acted like I'd done something wrong.

But while I was encouraged, through their words and their example, to not cover up my body or be embarrassed by it, I never actually learned that there is something healthy and sexual about our physical forms. Rarely did they kiss. I don't remember them even ever holding hands. I have one traumatic memory of wandering into the living room in the middle of the night and seeing them kissing and canoodling on the couch. When both acted even more horrified than I was, I knew that I'd seen a bad thing.

By the night of the couch mishap, I was already working through some other issues. A year before, at the age of nine, I started to develop the first signs of breasts. My mother, who had never filled much more than a training bra, rushed me to our pediatrician, Dr. Gaskins, alarmed that her little girl was going to look like a *Playboy* playmate before high school. He reassured her, saying that even when girls began developing early on, it didn't mean that they are destined to be voluptuous. She felt better, happy that she wasn't losing her little girl already. But I didn't. Even though I couldn't quite grasp what was happening, I knew that a corner had been turned. My body was doing something that it wasn't supposed to be doing, and my mother hadn't been accepting or pleased. She'd been nervous.

A year later, when I got my period, I was the nervous one. I wouldn't discuss it with anyone, and I cringed with embarrassment if a Kotex commercial came on TV in front of my father, who was still recovering from my having asked him the definition of "hard on," a phrase pulled from Judy Blume's *Then Again, Maybe I Won't*. I read in amazement other young adult novels of girls rushing home, hoping and praying that their underwear would be stained with red, unable to comprehend what pleasure they could find in this painful mess.

By age ten, I'd already been tainted by too much TV watching. A made-for-television movie called *Something About Amelia* had managed to inflict enough damage to my psyche that I'm still working it all out. The film was about a father, played by everybody's favorite guy behind the bar, Ted Danson, who was raping his twelve-year-old daughter, Amelia. Her mother, played by Glenn Close, didn't want to believe that her husband could be capable of such things, making for two hours' worth of conflict, confession, and resolution. I, who had disobeyed orders not to watch it, was captivated and horrified. Horrified not so much for poor Amelia but by the idea that a man that I knew—my father, an uncle, an older cousin—could want me like that. I went on-guard, unable to sleep well for months.

I never talked to anyone, not even my mother, about my fears. She had always prided herself on keeping the lines of communication open to discuss anything, yet I was still woefully ignorant of so much. Even though she'd brought me in to every doctor's appointment when she was pregnant with my brother, and even though she'd sat down with me and read through a very technical book on "where babies come from," I knew nothing about sexuality. Sex, yes. Sexuality, no. I could tell you, in textbook terms, about the egg and sperm and ovulation and cycles. But nothing as to what it felt like to want to kiss someone or be held in their arms or even what it meant to just be horny. I couldn't fathom the existence of sexual desire. Or at least I couldn't until *Something About Amelia* came along and filled in the gaps with the worst.

The fear put in my heart by that movie was compounded in later years with an uneasiness that sex was forbidden and taboo. In the absence of seeing adults I knew acting as sexual people, I instead watched enough television and movies to know that it was dirty. Or at least I tried to watch. Anytime there was a flash of breast on a screen, my mother's hand went over my face, leaving me achingly curious about what was happening on the other side of her five-finger barrier. During what I assumed was a XXX sex scene in *Purple Rain*, she practically leapt from her movie theater seat to get over to me and cover my eleven-year-old eyes. Years later, when I saw a late-night cable showing of the movie, I discovered that Prince's worst offense had been feeling up

Apollonia on top of her clothes, apparently enough to raise the ire of my mother the censor.

As lustful activity was being kept from me, I was simultaneously easing into my role as The Good Girl. The concept of unconditional love was sort of foreign to me. Without anyone having told me, I believed that what made me so lovable was the fact that I didn't really get in the way too much. I thought I'd sealed my place as Wonderful Daughter and Favorite Grandchild by being an excellent student who always did what was expected with minimal back talk. So it makes sense, in retrospect, that as my body developed hills and curves—all things connected to a "sinful" sexuality—I grew ashamed.

Matters got worse on the day my parents decided that, at thirteen, I was too old for them to chauffeur me everywhere. So I went through the rite of passage of many a Philadelphia youth before and after me. I got my first Transpass, an absurdly decorated rectangle of hologrammed plastic that provides unlimited access to the city's mass transit system. I remember thinking it was freedom, this being able to go wherever I wanted (provided I reported each new destination to my mother in advance and made it home by dinner). What I hadn't bargained for, as I euphorically swiped my card from turnstile to turnstile, was the new world of Men on the Street.

To reach the el train—my passport to school, ballet class, the mall, and the park where I wasted hours of my life—required a four-block walk. Ten minutes, seven if I really stepped to it. But some days it felt like an endless stretch.

You see, I have nipples that are always hard. Back in those days, I never left the house without a hoodie or sweater I could throw on if I saw a congregation of men on a corner. And for good measure, I also took to rounding my shoulders so they wouldn't seem so prominent.

Even before I had breasts, I could tell you about hard nipples. It was because my parents and I were big fans of the TV show *WKRP in Cincinnati*. One night my mother, who I'm sure would never remember this, said, "Loni Anderson's headlights are always on! Something must be wrong with her or else they're fake."

My mother never used proper terms—I was raised in a world of "pee pees" and "willies" and "headlights." But what she'd said stuck in my mind for other reasons, because I didn't understand what could go wrong with "headlights" to make them look like that. A few years later, I felt cursed when it happened to me, when no matter how high the thermostat and cold my libido, my nipples were there for the looking. It made walking down the street a nightmare. Holding a conversation with a male was even worse. Having breasts is enough to spark a sexual thought in most men's brains. Having breasts that look like you just ran ice cubes over them is like pushing the "play" button on a porno. Now, as an adult, I in turn have become the Nipple Police. I know that on *Friends*, Jennifer Aniston is often, in the words of one of my guy friends, "smuggling raisins." It's one of the reasons I like her so much. She goes into millions of homes at full salute. Hell, I just have to get to the corner store.

But back in middle and high school, I didn't have a famous celebrity example to console me (no girl running from her sexuality wants to be like Loni Anderson). What I did have were dirty old men licking their lips as I scampered by. One day I even had a pack of eight-year-olds surrounding me as I walked to the el, egging each other on to, "Touch her titties! Oooh, look at how they bounce!" One went so far as to touch my butt, until I turned around so fast and looking so enraged that they ran off. It was like being attacked by a swarm of mosquitoes—quick moving, annoying, and determined.

Each encounter took a little more out of me. My characteristic gait lost a little of its bounce as I made every conscious effort to keep my breasts from bobbing around. I envied women who seemed to have those breasts that looked like 1950s pinup models', the cone-shaped ones that wouldn't move an inch. Somehow, no matter what kind of bra I put on, mine were full of pep. When the requisite hoodie wasn't covering up my chest, it was securely tied around my waist to camouflage my behind from peering eyes.

I would watch other girls strut down the street in tight jeans and lots of attitude, daring men to look at them, wanting to take part in the sexual exchange that can happen with a stranger on the street. I wondered what they knew that I didn't, how it could be fun to banter with a man who had just finished whistling at the woman five feet ahead of you. I wanted to exchange my sullied feelings with their sure bravado.

The sidewalks and subway stations of my city weren't the only places that I was subject to unasked-for commentary, but they were the worst. At school, I'd had my bra strap popped as I walked down the hall and even the whole bra unhooked in the time that it took to pass someone at a locker. My butt had been pinched, my cup size had been guessed at, yet none of that really made such a big difference.

A boy in my classroom was on my level. I knew his name; he knew mine.

We had probably hung out, had a conversation, shared a laugh. So in the confused world of pubescent hormones, his horniness was not an insult. However, the man on the street who didn't know me had zero right, as far as I was concerned, to comment on my body. A stranger was barred from being able to stammer, "Mmm, mmm, mmm" as he shook his head from side to side and looked at my passing ass. It's acceptable to nod your approval of a nice car or a cute dog out for a walk. I couldn't understand what made it all right to act those same ways, and worse, when dealing with another human being.

Phyllis Weinberg was the reason why it was so terrible to hear a "Psst! Psst!" from a passerby on the street. She was my fourth-grade teacher whom I thought was the coolest lady in the world because she gave impromptu yoga classes if the weather cancelled recess and taught us anticapitalist, hippie folk songs in between science lessons. It was Mrs. Weinberg who covered the Salem witch trials during social studies class, also taking time to get in a word or two about how a woman suspected of adultery could be dunked in water or publicly whipped in Colonial America.

During the time I was her student, I drove everyone around me crazy, demanding answers for why a man could wield such power over a woman's body and behavior, yet she couldn't reciprocate. "Things were different back then," was the popular reply from my parents and other older adults. And I believed it until a few years later, as I walked to the train and had to endure whatever was being said by the men I'd pass. From what I could see, a woman still didn't have a whole lot of control over what a man, any man, could say about her.

The obvious imbalance of power, and the fact that I was on the losing side, was infuriating. I would watch my mother for behavior cues, how she always smiled, said thank you, acting as if she wasn't bothered in the least by a man wolf-whistling in her direction. At first I admired her congeniality, but one day, as a hotheaded sixteen-year-old, I decided I'd had enough of that, too. "Why?" I wanted to know. "Why do you *have* to be nice to them? You didn't ask them to talk to you on the street!"

"Because you don't want them to think you have an attitude," my mother answered, looking at me like I was dense.

"Who cares? Why should I care what some man whom I don't know thinks about me? Does he care what I think about him talking to me?"

"If you just smile and say 'thank you' they'll leave you alone. Otherwise they'll get mad, might yell that you're being a bitch."

She didn't get it. I *was* being a bitch. If you don't get to be a bitch to a drunk guy who insists on sitting next to you on the bus, breathing in your face, asking for your number, then what's bitchiness for? If these men got to act however they wanted, then I wasn't going to censor my behavior.

My mother looked worried. And she should have, since underneath all my talk and righteous indignation, I was more than a little scared. Because as much as I believed that no random guy had a right to tell me what nice hips I had, I also knew that if they felt comfortable with that, they also might feel at ease putting their hands on me or cussing me out in public. With a tiny physical frame and just one fight under my belt (which I'd won only through aggressive wielding of a metal Holly Hobbie lunchbox), I was no match for anyone.

As my mom prayed that I didn't get myself hurt with my teeth-sucking and eye-rolling public persona, I was trying to get into college and out of Philadelphia. In 1991, at seventeen, I chose Barnard College, the all-women's undergraduate branch of Columbia University, and moved to New York City.

One week in the city and I felt free. Philly was a place where it was considered indecent to have a bra strap showing from under a tank top. I moved to Manhattan around the same time it was declared legal for women to go topless. Before Rudolph Guiliani became mayor and went on his Quality of Life crusade, mine greatly improved just by watching women of every shape, size, and color walk around as if they owned the place; they wore tank tops and minis with hard nipples and jiggly thighs.

Also out from the eyes of my family, I stopped feeling self-imposed pressure to appear virginal, even though I'd had sex months before high school graduation. Cropped tops and pants that fit replaced my baggy jeans and oversized sweaters. I felt a rush of adrenaline knowing I looked sexy when I'd walk through a club or even into a classroom. I was on a high— young, cute, and out too late in a city that I thought was a haven.

This Golden Era lasted for four years. Then I moved to an outer borough. In all fairness to Brooklyn, where I took up residence, I had run into knucklehead comments on the street before graduating from college and leaving the protected grounds of Columbia University. But when I moved to "Prospect Heights" (a neighborhood newly coined by Realtors attempting to charge higher rents on Crown Heights properties), they became a daily occurrence.

My apartment building was one block in either direction from a subway stop, the dividing line between the Prospect Heights of the future and the

Crown Heights of right now. If I headed out the door and to my right for the local train, I passed where the Whites lived, those co-ops and condos that had long been gentrified because of their proximity to Park Slope. To my left was the express line and West Indian and African American men leaned against their cars, enjoying the sights, and boys propped on stoops, hanging with friends, talking shit, and looking at the ladies.

Suddenly my socially ambiguous wardrobe (am I headed to the club or to the office?) was calling all sorts of attention to me. My Barnard fierce feminist rhetoric ("This is my body—I can dress however and do what I want with it, and no one has the right to say or do anything!") sounded empty and naïve. I had to admit to myself that I had spent the past four years living in a bubble, by day going to an elite college and at night rolling with a pack of women around the streets of the Village and Soho. Now I was alone, just trying to get to work, but my platform shoes, navel-baring shirts, and, yes, especially my hard nipples, were not making it easy. The hoodies came back out, and my shoulders regained their familiar roundedness.

Until the day of the midtown pussy talker. While definitely not the scariest thing I'd encountered (that would have been when drunk neighborhood guys decided to have their pit bull chase me because I wouldn't stop to talk to them at I A.M.), it was the final straw. I'd had enough of feeling preyed upon, of somehow being forced to accept that it was just a way of life to hear these catcalls, or *piropos* in Spanish, when I was minding my business on the street.

Knowing there was nothing I could do to silence the men, I decided to work on myself. I tried to figure out why I was so upset, what made me so fearful that I turned it into hatred deep enough to want to shoot a man I didn't know. I looked into what my own sexuality meant to me now that I was a person actually having sex and not just an adolescent sneaking to watch it on cable. And I figured out that a sizable percentage of what made me feel desirable came from attention—the nonpornographic variety—that I got on the street, on the subway, and in other public places. I felt like a Shakespearean character, hating that which I fed upon. *Ay, there's the rub.*

All this work on myself would have been beautiful and positive and life-affirming if I hadn't developed an even worse attitude toward the men who opened their mouths to shout out (or sometimes suggestively murmur) obscene come-ons. Fear was replaced with righteous disgust. That second summer in Brooklyn, just weeks after the Pussy Affair, I was approached by a grown man riding around on what looked like a child's bike. He was determined to ride alongside me as I walked home from the subway, telling me I was pretty, asking did I have a boyfriend, could he be my friend? Nothing I said, and no amount of uppity attitude that I gave off, seemed to deter him. Finally, playing what I thought would be my trump card, I lied and told this man, who seemed to be at least thirty, that I was sixteen. I just knew that if he believed me that he'd look alarmed and pedal away. Instead, he seemed even more excited, wanting to know when he could call me that my mom or dad wouldn't be home.

For the rest of the summer, I was determined to see at what age a man would run scared in the other direction. So each time someone insisted on engaging me in conversation as I went on my way, I waited for them to ask me my age, always telling them something years below the jailbait cutoff. Because I look the same today as I did in high school photographs, each man believed what I told them, but none, not even the two who thought they were kicking it to a thirteen-year-old, were turned off. My fury knew no bounds after that season. The world, I declared, was full of pedophiles and perverts, ready to pounce on a preteen.

As winter came around and catcallers headed inside their apartments, I had more downtime to think about my hostility. I even spent some time wrestling with whether I was afraid of Black men, whether I had bought into the stereotypes so entrenched in the culture about their predatory natures and animal lusts.

One unseasonably warm day, and one bold-talking White boy, showed that if anything, I was letting the brothers off easy. As I walked past a group of White guys standing outside of Tower Records in the Village talking about the new Biggie album, one leaned toward me, lowered his voice, and said, "Hey, brown sugar, can I talk to you?"

Two minutes before a similar group of Black men had interrupted their conversation so that one of them could ask if he could get a lick (of what he hadn't made clear). But this "brown sugar" thing was the more unforgivable of the two. I was shocked and furious well beyond what the comment warranted. I looked at him like he was spit on the sidewalk and walked away full of righteous indignation. I blamed hip-hop and White Privilege and everything in between for making him think it was okay to talk to me. I even considered going back and telling the Black guys what had happened, knowing they weren't going to go for some White boy acting up with one of "their" women. Didn't he know that we may go to the same clubs and listen to the same music and even might be friends but it is not okay to cross the line? That somehow a real ignorant thing from a Black man was better than a slightly off-color comment by a White guy, because his statement would be supported by a history of plantation rape and jungle fever fantasies?

That was in 1996. Since then I have been followed up (and back down) the Spanish Steps in Rome by two Italian men telling me I was their "chocolate Madonna." I've been mistaken for a prostitute as I sat having dinner with girlfriends in Marrakech and spit on by teenage boys for daring to ignore their advances during eight particularly intense days in Morocco. And on a good note, I have also, thanks to having surpassed the three-decade mark, been greeted with "Excuse me, ma'am" from young men who just wanted to tell me that I was "looking beautiful today."

And with these, and a host of other day-to-day exchanges with men on the street, I wish that I could say I had learned to let the more unsavory and most objectifying statements roll off my back. But the truth is that, in place of developing a harder skin, around 1999, I simply took myself out of the running.

Much of the decision was made by outside factors. My feet began complaining loudly each time I put them in a pair of heels and insisted they walk me around the city. So I declared myself a wearer of flat shoes and $10 flip-flops only, drastically reducing my on-the-street appeal. As I was adopting a new, sportier look, high school girls were trying to look like women in music videos and *Sex and the City*. I was edged out by a rainbow gathering of Britney Spears and Beyoncés with more put-on sex appeal than men in cars, Starbucks windows, and construction sites could handle. I, in the latest Pumas, was dull by comparison. And finally, I got a car, removing myself from the sidewalk culture under which *piropos* are allowed to flourish.

Yet every year on that first warm-weather day, when Manhattan-bound traffic forces me to leave the Mercury Sable at home, I must pray for a miracle. Reminding myself that I'm a grown woman and that my body is undoubtedly my own, I leave the hoodie in the closet and hope that a heartfelt, "Ay, mami," doesn't get me to dreaming about polishing my gun.

Ayana Byrd is a co-editor of *Naked*.

BLACK
FUZZY
THING

Asali Solomon

T̶ell yourself what you will. Everyone knows that the most valuable capital that a woman can possess is a beauty that other people agree on. But many women have to decide that they are beautiful in spite of what they've been told by high school boys, employers, and music videos. I did. I'm medium-height, dark-skinned, and thick around the middle, with flat, size nine, corn-flecked feet. I know I'm beautiful because I decided that this is the case. But sometimes I can't shake the sinking feeling that no one besides my parents and sister know it. With apologies to DuBois, I've raced past modern double consciousness right into the collective mental illness of postmodern multiconsciousness. I can see myself through the eyes of the brother in the obscenely shiny black Escalade who stares right through me, the White woman smiling at me curiously in the supermarket, and the

Mexican construction worker who leers at me with erotic hostility. Despite how I try to see myself, it sometimes catches me and takes my breath away that for most people I'm homely because I'm brown and nappy.

There is, however, one remarkable thing about me physically, and that is my hair. It is the thing that people most want to touch and talk about. I have indisputably beautiful dredlocks, thin, defined, falling to the middle of my back. I decided to grow them when I was twenty-one and newly out in the Real World. I wanted good-looking, hassle-free hair. I wanted a date (something I believe past styles had kept me from securing), but did not want a chemical straightener that wouldn't agree with me. So Roberta, my old loctician back in Brooklyn who started me seven years ago, taught me how to take care of my hair so well that people on the street here in Oakland (and there in Philadelphia, Atlanta, and Baltimore) think that I should be doing their hair as well.

People love my locks so much that I don't feel like it's my hair. Because *my* hair is an ill-fated high school perm that I could never get to hold a recognizable style or grow into a respectable ponytail. My hair is a gangly natural that chunked up into a kinky misery when I sweated at middle school dances. My hair is the super-close-cut natural that I loved, but suspect kept me from having a date all through college, being heterosexual and all. And my hair is the thin, shoulder-length, shake-able extension braids that I liked wearing but were literally not my hair.

But this remarkable hair of mine, it plagues me. It asks me questions, like What do you love about me now? Do you like the geometry of my lines? Do you love the different reds and blacks that mingle at surprising intervals? Do you love the nappy edges that you beat back with your endless twisting? Or do you like that I hang down like a White girl's?

Uh-oh.

See, I know how I *should* feel about Black hair, Black people, and Black me. I am the firstborn Swahili-named daughter of two righteous Black folks of the '60s from West Philly, who got married in dashikis and afros and taught me that a Black man invented the traffic light, and possibly electricity itself. I'm the daughter of Brother Sol and Sister Rochelle, who told me early on (maybe too early, my therapist says) about slavery and the assassination of Malcolm X, about the once and future glory of The Continent, and about the mess that Europe has made of the world. My mother and father made a Black space for themselves away from White Jesus, in a house filled with ebony statues with embarrassing protuberances. They made a Kwanzaa-friendly space for my sister and me and outlawed the watching of *Dukes of Hazzard* (too pro–good ol' boys), *Gimme a Break* (too pro-Mammy), and *Good Times* (too pro-Sambo).

The politics of beauty were symbolized in my home by pictures of smooth-headed, tall Massai women cut from Unicef calendars and a large art photo called *Rudy*, featuring a Black woman with cornrows that stuck straight up with puffy little ends. They were also represented by the short natural that my mother has worn my entire life. I remember being young (not quite ten years old) and precocious at the supermarket. I had just inexplicably learned the phrase "beauty standards." While we were rolling down the hair products aisle, I asked my mother, "So you don't follow White beauty standards, huh?" As if it were the least complicated thing in the world, the most natural position in this majority racist country, she said, "No."

I have come to understand that raising my sister and me to understand racial consciousness as a moral imperative is not as easy as my parents perhaps imagined. I mean, we did live in the world! We had television; I remember hearing the theme songs to *Wonder Woman* and *Charlie's Angels*, quietly being indoctrinated to dig olive brunette Linda and tawny blonde Farrah. We also saw Disney movies: *Snow White*, *Sleeping Beauty*, and *Cinderella*—brunette, blonde, and blonde.

So is it any wonder the way I remember kindergarten? I went to an "independent" school with the children of White hippies and professors at the University of Pennsylvania. I recall being surrounded with White girls on the nubby rug where we read stories and sang songs. When I look back, I cannot see myself, but instead a ring of blonde/brunette girls with high-pitched voices and an awful blur, a black fuzzy thing on the rug.

Though I went to school with Black kids from first through fourth grade, I took the black fuzzy feeling with me. It didn't help that the short, thumbsucking tyrant who ruled our class had one of the few perms (and the first pair of leather pants I've ever seen). Then, during some poignant middle school years, I went to school with rich White girls in the suburbs. It was there that I willfully changed my mind and, stopping short of full resolution, began feeling definitely unpretty instead of merely invisible. The solution to this new discomfort came to me in fantasies where I led a fawning group of followers down the stately hallway from the dining room to the classroom. I couldn't have articulated why at the time, but the fantasy me had mixed-girl hair.

I loved it! My dream hair floated and billowed and could be tied up in a spirited ponytail. It framed my face in a sympathetic way. It was yielding and giving—not the nappy mess that erupted at the school dance. It was the hair that would finally get me noticed. For I have to blame my real-life hair for that Friday night in the gym, seventh grade, when a tall blonde guy from our "brother" school said to me, "That guy over there wants to dance with you!" with a smirk that he must have known I would see.

With mixed hair in kindergarten, I could have been a Black, flowing thing instead of a blur on the rug. And I could have floated out of range of so much pain.

If you are a brown, nappy girl, there are many things you might want to change, so much capital you do not have. I could have wished to be light-skinned. I could have wished to be White (may God and my parents strike me down!). That one day in seventh grade when Heather asked me to pucker up so she could laugh at my full lips—I could have wished those suckers away. But for a Black woman, it is most often her hair that catches her racial imagination. Her hair holds what she loves and hates about herself and shapes her experience of family, lovers, and friends. It forms her most intimate experiences of gender, race, social class, the humid summer, and the ocean. Hair is not only a marker of racial difference and gender-specific beauty, but the marker that seems most malleable. Black women spend thousands of dollars and hours to achieve dreams of love and acceptance through their hair. All things are possible through a tame "kitchen" (the rebellious, quickest-to-kink-up area at the nape of the neck), a few more inches, or the illusion of loose crinkles.

Living out my parent's politics as a girl meant that my sister and I could not get our hair straightened until high school, and even then my mother was mournful. Perming your hair was trying to make it look White, giving into the designs of the Evil Empire.

To continue sketching out my idea of this problem, I need to say something real ugly. In its natural state, as far as most people are concerned, Black women's hair is unpresentable. In the early '90s, I was growing out my short hair, as were my roommates, who also had short, natural hair. Each morning we wet and gelled our hair, leaving the house in winter with semi-organic Jheri Curls, affecting an unnatural natural look. We never discussed the water and gel. We never mentioned the shameful drips on our necks. For us at a feminist college, brilliant Black women who shunned the perm and lived in New York in the goddamn 1990s, our hair in its natural state was unpresentable. It's true that before the catastrophe of European imperialism, the African impulses of which I am aware were to style and adorn the hair with beads, clay, braids, and jewels. But that was and is building on the existing beauty, not obliterating or disguising its very essence. I don't believe that this was the same as keeping your dredlocks neat because you live in fear of the fuzzy edges, or the same as sporting wet, gelled hair in February down bone-chilling Riverside Drive.

Recently I was loving myself in the mirror and my hair suddenly asked me this: "Would you like me better if I was Aaliyah's?" (It was, of course, before the singer died.) I found that her long, full, relaxed head of hair gave me aches. The beauty of *that* hair made me hurt with admiration. And want to hurt myself. "Would you like me better," my hair still asks, "if I was not neat dredlocks that any kinky girl could get, but a soft, blurry swish of obscenely shiny black?"

But I can't be watching BET to get my self-esteem on. I've got to get my mind right, like my friend Antoinette says, and find in my soul the right answer to all the questions my hair asks. Or do I?

I often wish my mother had thought longer about it that day in the supermarket, maybe told me more of what she went through in the pre-afro '60s when she had a thin perm, split ends, and a goofy smile. I often wish I had told her more of how I felt about myself, and not only about the day when I was twelve and the Black boys in McDonald's hooted approvingly at my friend with the perm and barked at me. I wish someone had told me that the only thing as torturous as holding a standard of beauty you can never achieve is holding a standard of consciousness that is proving impossible to maintain.

Asali Solomon is an assistant professor of English at Washington & Lee University. She is currently completing a short-story collection and a novel, both to be published by Fararr, Straus and Girroux.

THE CURSE
OF IDA BELL

Lori L. Tharps

Photo by G. Giraldo.

The story starts with my mother. She hadn't yet set foot on the earth, but her destiny was already sealed. Still developing in utero, my mother was witness to her father's infidelity. Actually, it was my grandmother who caught her husband cheating with Ida Bell, that no-good whore, and it nearly broke her in two. Rather than wallow in shame and defeat, my grandmother's fighting spirit took over. She caught that trampy Ida Bell unawares one day and chased her through an empty field of Mississippi red dirt, brandishing her husband's shotgun. She threatened to kill Ida Bell if she so much as came close to my grandfather again. Believing she had settled things, my grandmother was horrified to give birth four months later to a dark little girl she named Quincy John (after the president) who looked, in her mind, remarkably like Ida Bell instead of her other cinnamon-colored daughters.

"You've been marked," my grandmother told her child as soon as she was old enough to comprehend things like "fate" and "tragedy." "It's 'cause of what I did, but you got the punishment. You look just like that ol' Ida Bell, and you'll probably turn out just like her, too. Nothing but a whore."

My mommy spent her childhood, first in Egypt, Mississippi, and then up north in Milwaukee, Wisconsin, trying desperately to outsmart the curse of Ida Bell. She worked twice as hard as any of her ten sisters in school to ensure that she would never have to rely on her body for success. She dressed conservatively and kept her hair straight and plain. Eventually Quincy became "the smart one" instead of "the marked one" and was only referred to as "the dark one" or "ink spot" in sudden fits of anger.

When Quincy had just finished being a child at age nineteen, my grandmother died—officially of a stroke, unofficially of a broken heart because my grandfather never stopped chasing women—but not before she imparted some important life lessons to her daughter. Red nail polish was for hussies. Only whores didn't wear slips. And more than anything, my mother was told to find a husband lighter than herself or else her children would hate her.

So at twenty-one, Quincy married my father, a high-yellow naval officer with middle-class dreams and fleeting celebrity as one of *Ebony* magazine's bachelors of the month. One year later, my sister was born, followed by me and my brother. Then my mother was done with making babies, and it was my turn to grow up.

✳   ✳   ✳

Because my mother lived her childhood in constant fear of sliding into a swamp pit of loose living, her parenting philosophy for her own daughters fell into the "I ain't raising no hoes" camp as well. On a conscious level, as a mental health professional and a nurse, she knew that the curse of Ida Bell wasn't real. But the lessons learned from her own mother were deeply ingrained in her psyche.

My mother had a plan for her daughters. My sister and I were to flaunt our intelligence and cover our asses. She never told us to hide our bodies, but it was implied. Hide it from whom or what, I was never sure, but the message was clear. In the meantime, no red toenail polish, because that was for whores. No ankle bracelets. Same reason. Earrings only after age thirteen, and I knew not to even think about multiple piercings.

That's not to imply that my childhood was strict. Indeed, my mother seemed to take great pride in raising little girls who could tickle grown-ups with our outrageous stories and opinions. If there'd been a slogan to announce her intentions, it would have read, "Be known for your mind, darling, not your body."

Because I was encouraged to be clever and talented, I took acting and singing lessons, piano, swimming, ballet, and gymnastics. I concentrated on being fabulous and didn't much think about being cute.

It didn't take me too long to learn my place in the cosmic scheme of life. By the time I hit the seventh grade, my cousin, who was the same age, had a boyfriend. I had made the cross-country team. Being the lone Black female in my class and in the neighborhood only added to my lack of interest in getting noticed for any aspect of my body. As I saw it, assimilation required disappearing into a vast sea of White. Showcase hairstyles would require a lecture on Black Hair Care 101. Tight pants would call for a level of self-confidence I have never possessed. And truth be told, there were no sexy Black females to emulate even if I wanted to flaunt my assets. Sex and the Black female in my 1980s Midwestern, suburban worldview was limited to negative stereotypes of ghetto-living welfare queens.

Add to this "body-as-an-afterthought" scenario the fact that there were no Black boys at my school on which to pin my affections. One bad experience on the jungle gym in the first grade, vying for the attention of a White boy, had been enough (Brian Taylor said he liked me, too, but because I was Black he had to chose Hilary Harris to be his girlfriend). I declared myself the type who would wait until college to find a boyfriend, and meanwhile stayed focused on being talented and smart over sexy and stupid. To satisfy adolescent, hormone-fueled urges, I read a lot of juicy Harlequin paperbacks and imagined my adult future would magically unfold like a romantic fairy tale.

By the time I made it to college, I was ready to test my mother's theories against what the rest of the world was offering: sex! sex! and more sex! Surely my roommate and her friends, who made slutty look admirable, must know something my mother didn't. Besides, despite my best attempts to downplay my body, like wearing pajamas to class and calling a baseball hat a hairstyle, I was receiving attention from boys . . . and men! Sometimes it was a catcall in the street; other times it was the earnest proposal of a boy who wanted to be my special friend. Lewd comments made me feel as dirty as my mother intimated, but when a nice boy made his feelings known, I enjoyed the tingle up my spine.

So a month into school, I hopped on a bus and went to the mall. I bought clothes that would make my mother blush: my first miniskirt, thigh-high patent leather boots, and fake silk panties. Back at the dorms, however, I felt so guilty that I bagged up my naughty acquisitions and returned them. Despite my best efforts to dismiss my mother's lessons, they had shaped my concept of appropriate dress and behavior.

Once I accepted my fate as an eighteen-year-old who didn't feel right showing skin, I stopped trying to rebel. My body and I developed a mutually beneficial relationship. I didn't love or hate it. I fed it and gave it water and rest. I never abused it with drugs or alcohol, although sometimes I did feed it McDonald's french fries and Taco Bell. In other words, I would treat it with decency and it would stay in the background until called upon to perform.

Before college, I didn't think of myself as sexual or beautiful. I had no idea what a clitoris was for and still believed that my bountiful Black booty was something no man would want. But over the next four years continuing into my twenties, however, I threw aside the Harlequins and started exploring my sexuality with real live human beings. I began to realize my body could, in fact, be an object of desire. Men I trusted and adored told me I was beautiful, and I believed them. My future husband couldn't say enough about the wonders of my delightfully delicious ass. And as I traveled further and further away from my Milwaukee roots, I was exposed to more Black women who were not afraid to flaunt their beauty and their bodies and still managed to command respect. I was not a woman transformed, but I was definitely on a path of self-discovery.

By the time I turned twenty-eight, I was happily married to the man who loved my butt because he promised to do so forever and ever, Amen. Two years later we decided to start a family. Before creating a new life we discussed money, education, race (my husband is from Spain), and how our lives would change. Never once did I consider how pregnancy would alter my relationship with my body.

One month into our efforts, I was "with child." I couldn't wait to attain that mythical glow. Just the thought of a human being growing inside of my slightly neglected body was enough to make me sign up for yoga classes, eat only organic produce, and stay away from those french fries. For the first time in my life, I vowed to pamper and celebrate my body.

Instead, the first three months proved anticlimactic. My breasts got a little bigger. My stomach stuck out a bit. The queasiness and exhaustion that mark many women's first trimester hardly affected me. Soon I reverted to my old ways of thinking, even applauding my body for being "strong enough" to create life without interrupting our daily routine.

At four months, my husband took a Polaroid of my stomach for posterity. Looking at it together, we could barely make out a bulge, and I felt conflicted. On the one hand, I was ready to show the world I was having a baby, ready for the perks pregnant women often receive, like guaranteed seats on the subway, and the freedom to eat like a pig in public without receiving reproachful glances from strangers.

On the other hand, I was glad that my body was not spreading in unsightly ways. When people would comment that from the back I didn't even look pregnant, I took it as a compliment.

Around month five it all changed. My "condition" (or rather my stomach) exploded, and my body was getting me noticed. How could it not, with twenty extra pounds of baby weight spread across my 5'3" frame?

But instead of euphoria at my baby's prearrival status, I felt embarrassment. Everywhere I went I sensed the prying gaze of strangers. *Were they judging me?* I wondered, as my ever-expanding belly displayed my personal affairs. On the streets of Manhattan, in the subways, at restaurants, I felt transparent. Was it paranoia to think, as a White stranger's eyes traveled across my body, that they were imagining another Black female who was just thoughtlessly fucking? This was my, or rather my mother's, worst nightmare visited upon me—being mistaken for a whore.

I tried to remind myself, as I caught one more questionable look from a White passerby, that not everyone equated my pregnancy with wanton sexual behavior. Yet I knew that in the minds of many people, Black women—beginning with the Venus Hottentot and ending with Lil' Kim—are all sex fiend negresses who cannot keep our legs together.

As much as I blamed racism for my discomfort, I also held my body responsible. It was as if it had mutinied, forgetting about our pact to look out for each other. Contrary to the prevailing myth that pregnancy is a magical time in a woman's life, mine was more like disintegration into physical disorder. Hair sprouted in strange places, massive zits took up residence on the tip of my nose, and my feet and ankles were so swollen that the only shoes that fit were a pair of gaudy red slides I bought on a dare the previous summer. And these were just the visible problems. There was also my leaky bladder, neverending gas, and hemorrhoids. I felt completely unattractive and quite powerless.

It had been my intention to present a picture of earth-mother-goddess—something to make my ancestors proud. But as I got bigger and bigger, I wanted nothing more than to hide. I was just so *huge*. Small children "accused" me of being pregnant, while adults took to stopping their cars to get a better look at my supersized stomach. When my mother saw me at the end of my eighth month, she pointed and laughed, "You look like you swallowed a watermelon and it tipped over!" Seeing my reflection in a mirror or store window even I was startled at times.

My swollen form, I decided, had come to define me. I was no longer Lori the writer. Or Lori the funny Black girl, or even Lori the wife. At an impromptu reunion with some college friends, while everyone else got asked about their jobs, love lives, and plans for graduate school, inquiries into my life revolved around my stomach. And that is when I realized how much I had taken for granted the ability to neutralize my body. I was never fat or skinny, which allowed me to define myself based on career, fashion sense, or even just a hairstyle. I'd once had the privilege of presenting whatever image I wanted to the world based on any number of factors. Now, lugging around a baby, I no longer had that option.

Interestingly, many of my White girlfriends were overjoyed to show off their rotund bellies, reveling in what they perceived as the positive attention from strangers. I was accused of being oversensitive to the probing questions and predictions of due dates by random shop clerks and elevator operators. "Don't you think most people have a soft spot for pregnant women?" they would ask me. "But I don't want to be thought of as a 'pregnant woman,'" I'd whine back. I wanted to be known for my mind, darling, not my body.

Just as I was about ready to pop, I became too tired to fight the inevitable. I made it up in my mind that there was no point in bemoaning my fate. I chose to get pregnant and, soon enough, I wouldn't be pregnant anymore. It was as simple and as difficult as deciding to stop smoking. The act may be difficult, but the decision was easy.

On the morning of one of the first hot summer days, I was looking for something to wear. Rather than squeezing into one of my usual disguises, an oversized shirt and sweat pants, I grabbed one of my husband's sleeveless undershirts. It was tight around the tummy but it was cotton and allowed my skin to breathe. Gazing in the mirror, I laughed out loud, knowing there was no way to hide this body. Adding a colorful peasant skirt and my sassy red slides, I felt earthy, womanly, and ready to greet the world.

As I hit the pavement with all my business showing, I thought, *Curious onlookers be damned!* And yes, people stared and honked at me from their cars. And yes, older Black women swore on their lives I was having twins. But I kept it in perspective: this was just one part of a long journey into motherhood. Although I still wished I could walk down the street all *incognegro* and inconspicuous—twenty-nine years with the curse of Ida Bell hanging over your head is hard to shake, but at least I felt like I wrestled back control of the situation. My body and I were at peace again.

Lori L. Tharps is a writer, teacher, and mother who lives in Philadelphia with her husband and two sons. She is the co-author of *Hair Story: Untangling the Roots of Black Hair in America.*

HO GEAR

Beverly Smith

As told to Ayana Byrd and Akiba Solomon

Photo courtesy of Beverly Smith.

I was the first girl in my neighborhood to wear Spandex. At thirteen, the parents around my way in Harlem had already started saying I was going to be a whore. I hadn't had sex, hadn't done anything, except that year I wore heels with my Easter outfit. So at fifteen, when I got a boyfriend and lost my virginity and started wearing Lycra, you should have heard the whispers of the moms.

It wasn't until my boyfriend that I had given any thought to my body. Before that, I lived in the shadow of my older sister. I was always cute or whatever, but compared to Stephanie, I had no butt. She'd a huge one since she was a little girl. In fear of aggressive men and potential rapists, my mom made her wear girdles when she was just eight. I, on the other hand, was skinny with no breasts, right up until age thirteen.

But this guy, whom I ended up dating for seven years, would say things like, "You have a nice shape, you should show it off." We would go shopping and he would pick out clothes that he thought would look good on me. I liked the attention at first but was shy. Then, after a while, I really looked in the mirror and thought, *That does look good.* And that's how it started. My first Spandex outfit was a white capri legging with a white silk miniskirt and a little red-and-white Spandex top from Betsey Johnson. It was very Madonna-esque, even though she wouldn't be popular for a couple more years. You could call that outfit a Jr. Beginner. Eventually things evolved into me wearing orange hotpant catsuits, popping out all over the place. Looking back, I admit it got insane.

But there was a proper time and place for my daring outfits. I would wear them to outings, special occasions. But honestly, you know that Black folks can turn anything into an outing. Which is why there was the day that I wore a pair of cream Spandex leggings, a midriff top, and heels to Universal Theme Park. What was I doing at an amusement park dressed like this?

Once, when I was twenty-two, just as an experiment, my friend and I decided to see what it would be like if we went to a party dressed like ladies in clothes we could wear to work. I wore a red silk skirt, red tight-fitting sweater, cream hosiery (it was, after all, the '80s), and red suede shoes. I've always gauged the success of an outfit by how many guys tried to talk to me, and using that criteria, we were still a hit. But nothing changed—by the next night we were back in the ho gear, counting our experiment as fun but nothing we were ready to adopt as permanent.

You know how some women say that they're wearing something but they don't want attention? I definitely dressed to get attention. *Oh, I'm super shy, I don't want anyone to notice me, but I'm wearing lace pants.* Come on, you're killin' me.

But believe it or not, even though I dressed like this, it was really tough for me to deal with catcalls and men thinking they could say whatever they wanted to me. I would get really upset, and curse men out. I've gotten into fights because a guy touched my butt in a club. I never considered dressing differently, because why should I have to? This is my body, I can showcase it however I want. Just because I'm wearing this does not give anyone the right to touch me. Just because I'll be the first to say "ho gear" doesn't mean I was a ho.

One of my rules has always been that if I am going to be in a relationship with a man, he has to get to know me very well before I will have sex with him. If I have a lot of respect for a man, if I think he's incredible, then he has to have the same degree of respect for me. My body was definitely a bonus, but it can't be that he wanted me just because I'm stacked up.

But if we aren't going to be in a relationship, then I don't really care what he thinks. What am I supposed to do? Go around and speak to every single person and explain, *No, you don't understand. I'm really bright and have it together.* It doesn't matter.

If I had to say how I got this way, it all goes back to Harlem, the Harlem that I grew up in. When I was younger, in the '80s and early '90s, it was all about a good ol' boomin' body. My friend Denise was light-skinned, with green eyes and long hair—the stereotype of what you would think men wanted. But she hated herself, hated how she looked. She wanted my body.

I lived across the street from the Dunbar Tavern and would look out the window at the people who went there. Now that I'm older, I know that many of the people who frequented the bar were "street people"—hustlers, drug dealers, number runners, and "loose women." But as a kid, their brightly colored clothes, fur coats, excessive amounts of gold jewelry—it all seemed to be the epitome of glamour. The women looked incredible to me—the way they dressed, their bodies, all of it. I was living around a bunch of Black folks with big old butts and they're considered the bomb, and I have a big butt, so how can I have any issues? So seeing Cheryl Tiegs in a Noxzema commercial on television never did anything to me. Even when I started working in the fashion industry and was around a lot of White people, I never thought that their ideal of beauty was beautiful. I mean, I could see beauty in a White woman, I knew that was someone's version of beauty, but it wasn't mine.

And my family never tried to stop me from dressing the way I did. When I would leave the house in a see-through shirt and lace pants with a visible thong, my mom would just say, "You look nice, baby." Actually, that was the outfit that was too much for my father. He simply said, "Bev, you've gone too far with this one."

He was probably right, because I was never one of those women who would shroud my body. I always saw it as one more asset to who I am as a person. I didn't go through a stage where I was insecure about it or ashamed. I never felt a way about being brown skinned or having short hair, none of it. I would look at myself and think, *Things could be better, but things could be worse and I'm a cute girl.* I kept it moving. You can be sick over a lot of shit. "Oh, I wish I was rich, look how rich they are." That's a poor way to live your life, wanting, wanting, wanting, coveting someone else's look. You gotta be happy with what you have.

Admittedly, I am extreme in my level of comfortability. I realized I was an exhibitionist when guys would tell me things like, "It's crazy—you can just get out of bed and go and get some water. Chicks be bringin' sheets." It never occurred to me to bring a sheet. Why would you bring the sheet? At home I am always naked. And I don't have any blinds or curtains, but I do have plenty of dance routines that I'm always practicing for when I go out to party at a club. And surprisingly, I don't even really wear lingerie. I'm more into no clothes, greased up and in a pump, a fierce heel.

If you look through our family photos, you can see that I'm not alone. In the family album, there's this one picture of my mom standing between me and my sister. We are both in our pajamas, and she's wearing baby blue lingerie. On top of the television in my parent's house is a picture of my Aunt Renie in a sheer pink babydoll nightie. Things like that send a certain message, like that it's okay to have your body on display.

Even parts of my body that someone else might worry about, I loved. Like my mound. Some women call it a stomach or even a pooch. But "pooch" sounds like "pouch," like something that can be taken off. I have been known to make men kiss my mound before I let them have sex with me. *Worship the mound, rub my mound,* I've told them. *Isn't it beautiful? Don't you love it?*

And men really do seem to love it. I've never gotten one negative comment from a guy about my body. There was this one time, I was in Miami at a music convention and Luke saw me and said, "You wanna be a dancer?" I said no, and he called one of his girls over and said, "Tell her how much money you make." I said, "I make good money now. Thanks, but no thank you, Mr. Luke."

Things like that don't really happen that much now, because I'm thirty-six and I've toned it down. My "grown and sexy" look is a lot of skirts, usually to the knee or a little above, major cleavage-bearing tops, and a very high stiletto. My body has also changed; I've gained some weight over the years. I don't know my measurements and don't weigh myself, but I'm not a size 2, 4, 6, or even an 8. I'm a good 10 or 12. But I still think I'm lovely—big titties, little waist, big ass—how are you losin' with that? Whatever angle you're coming from, there's something. Are you an ass man? I got that! Breast man? Got those, too!

Still, half those clothes I wore when I was younger I couldn't fit into anymore. Most of them are just not age-appropriate. So many women get caught up in just being defined by our body, but I always told myself that when I got older I was going to be less shocking and provocative. Don't get me wrong, I still have fun with my clothes. Like one night I had to go to a party and I was feeling very Vegas, very showgirl. So I decided to sprinkle body glitter in my cleavage when I got dressed to capture my brassy mood.

I've been at parties and had young women come up to me to say that I look amazing, and that feels so good to me. Well, I'm very comfortable being a grown ass woman. I'm thirty-six, and I'm blessed; why wouldn't I want to shout that to the rooftops? I go out to hip-hop clubs now because I love to dance, and the median age will be twenty-seven. Those girls are in better shape than I am; I have no illusions that I'm going to walk in the door and be the belle of the ball. But I'm not one of those women you see who has a scowl on her face, missing the spotlight now that she's one of the older women in a place. If I see a young lady and she's doin' it, I let her know, because I know how nice it makes me feel to get a sincere compliment from another woman.

This would all be an entirely different story if I were growing up now with this body because the support just isn't there. In the late '90s, I feel like Black women with big butts and titties went out of style. I think that guys still like chicks who look like me, but now, with the advent of videos, you see so many slender women getting play. I have to take it back to Harlem sometimes to give myself a boost of confidence. Every Saturday on 133rd Street, there's an African dance class full of women with every body you can imagine. And if you do something particularly good, the teacher will ask you to come up front. And some of these women are really big, and they are just loving themselves and loving the dancing and not self-conscious at all. It's like nothing you've ever seen. It's beautiful.

To this day, if I go uptown to a real gully spot, the way the people are dancing and rejoicing and enjoying themselves, it's amazing. And there are women looking all kinds of ways, and they are getting love and getting play. As long as she thinks she's a fly bitch, then cats are gonna think she's one, too. It's a sight to see. I love my folks.

Beverly Smith is an actress who has also worked in fashion advertising at Vibe and *Rolling Stone* magazines.

FOR COLORED GIRLS

Aminata Cisse

L ele, my caramel-colored best friend, is sitting next to me. We are deep in conversation with a palette of beige, tan, and birch-brown Black boys about the summer sun and complexions. I mention how much I enjoy tanning, and John, who is normally kind but now sneering, says, "You can get any darker than *that?*"

Everyone grows silent. I am paralyzed. John, whose Haitian Cuban skin is almost as dark as mine, has challenged the goodness of my Bajan Senegalese complexion. He has hit my weakness.

As I search for a clever way to defend myself, the conversation veers off to a more pleasant course. A few moments later, I leave the room, wearing shame on my face. John's insult remains unanswered.

NAKED

I have always been made aware of my skin color, even before I was cognizant of its meaning. In my otherwise vivid memory of childhood, I cannot name a defining moment or source of my color issues. I can remember feeling an ever-present ache of alienation and exclusion. I remember thinking that some people would not like me because of my complexion. But the details and dialogue are a blur of slights and verbal assaults on my ego.

I do know that in my own family, on summer trips to Barbados, I was made to feel invisible. My older cousins would rave about how pretty and cute the younger, lighter ones were but would never speak of my physical characteristics in any way. On these trips I remember feeling different in a bad way, marred by dark skin.

I can recall the junior high school sleepover where I was singled out as "the darky" for a round of unwarranted jokes about my complexion.

At the same time there was my mother, who would tell me that Black people were superior. She loved Malcolm X and routinely rhapsodized about the righteous struggles of our people throughout the African Diaspora. She'd implore me to embrace my heritage, to wear my skin like a cloak of soft velvet over my limbs. I wanted to love it for her. But I just didn't know how when everyone else seemed to be telling me that something was wrong.

Now, as a high school senior, most of my pain comes from relationships with males and their perception of me as a female. I go to parties and social gatherings where young men compliment me but never ask for my number. They gaze at my six-foot stature and my African features—full lips, slanted eyes, high cheekbones—and call me the "new ideal" of beauty. But they don't want to incorporate the dark brown girl into their day-to-day relations.

I've had boys call me pretty only to follow up with, "I could never see you with a boyfriend. You're just not the girlfriend type." If I didn't know better, perhaps these comments would make me feel like a divine, rarefied glass sculpture. But my girlfriends, who range in color from light- to brown-skinned, and I agree that young Black boys wear blinders that allow only light skin to filter through.

Karen, who has hair that grazes her butt and skin the color of butterscotch, tells me about the boys who respond to her standard question, "Why do you like me?" with, "Oh, you're light-skinned with long hair."

At parties, while I experience a shutout, I watch boys flock to Puerto Rican Lisa of the curly hair, light skin, and spastic movements.

I listen to close male friends continuously complain about the dull conversations they have with the generic-but-light-skinned girls they always choose.

When I watch rap videos, I feel myself physically deflate. Most of the representations of Black female beauty in these three-minute montages of the hip-hop high life are fair-skinned with European features. I understand that the girls are wearing makeup, have weaves, and enjoy the benefits of special lighting, but even if I had these advantages, I know could never live up to the one asset that never fails: light skin.

Yesterday, at Awards Night, I was honored for scoring high on the PSAT and I won a prize for A.P. American History. My best friend, Lele, didn't receive any. Today, as we stand at the drafting table in art class, she is behaving oddly—speaking loudly and acting extra "ghetto" for no reason. At first I ignore Aliya. But soon I grow tired of her antics, so when a White classmate gets up to fetch supplies, I leave her table and take her chair.

Aliya jokes that the White girl had better watch out for the "big Black girl" who has stolen her chair. Our tablemates, Alexandra, Nzingha, and Shawna, and I chuckle and continue painting. But Aliya can't seem to let it go. "Yeeaaahh Heather, you better beware of the BIG BLACK GIRL!"

On second reference to this threatening ape that is supposed to be me, I ask my best friend why she thinks it's necessary for her to repeat herself.

"Well, aren't you a darker complexion than everyone here?" she asks, smirking while she gestures toward Alexandra, Nzingha, and Shawna.

"Oooohhh!" the girls say, punctuating my best friend's blow.

As I sit there, my face melting in confusion, Aliya taunts me for becoming upset. "Oh, you tight!" she chants. "You tight! You tight!"

Finally, I recover my voice. "Yes, I *am* tight," I tell the girl with whom I have shared my fears, insecurities, and secrets. "I am tight because you are a *bitch!*"

These words end our friendship. The next day, at Shawna's Memorial Day barbecue, Lele tries to make amends. But Aliya has used the color card to embarrass me. It is an unforgivable offense.

There was a point in junior high school when I felt too Black to exist among Black people. I had been ostracized so often and felt so alienated that I wanted to move away from all that was us. If light-skinned people were so superior to me, I reasoned, why not go straight to the source of their genetic power? I decided to find my niche among White people.

My mom had tried to choose my path in life by telling me that Whites were the enemy. But during this period, I came to believe that she was holding out on me, that she had denied me an amazing, secret world.

Through television, movies, and radio, I was exposed to this world of sensitive soap stars; intelligent, interesting rockers; and quirky, liberal girls with glasses. Robert DeNiro and David Bowie—known for their admiration of deep-hued Black women—became my heroes. And in real life, when I'd venture into Manhattan, I'd see content dark-skinned women on the arms of bewitched White men. In their world, I wouldn't be "cute for a dark-skinned girl"; I'd be an exotic and a desired commodity.

This fantasy lasted until 2000, when, at fourteen, I attended a summer enrichment program at Dublin City University in Ireland. Out of 350 teenagers, I was the only Black person on the entire campus. Although I forged wonderful friendships, there was still an invisible barrier. At dances, I watched as my girlfriends paired off with boys in polo shirts named Dermott and Kieran. The young men would tell my friends how stunning I was, but I was always alone. Apparently I was an object for them to behold and quickly forget.

I returned to my Brooklyn neighborhood full of African American, Caribbean, European, and Latino people feeling less connected than ever. My complexion made me a second-class citizen among Blacks. My race made me an alien among Whites. I was between two walls with no way out.

*　*　*

In the most unexpected place, I find relief. I took my first trip to Senegal, my father's homeland, at eight. It was hell. I was peevish, immature, and overwhelmed by the raw reality that was West Africa. When I visited again at eleven, I contracted malaria and was bedridden for weeks. But on my third trip at age thirteen, I formed closer ties with my numerous cousins and realized the true beauty of Africa: its people.

Being in a place where everyone is tall and dark like me is balm for my soul. Dakar, where my father lives, is brimming with human electricity. Black people move and hustle but never in vain because they are moving and hustling among each other, the specter of a colonial master so far removed. In the country, on my grandparents' peanut and cassava farm, I smell the green of the land. I am enveloped by the winds and swallowed up in the pitch-black night sky.

In Senegal, I eat of the land, my father's land, my ancestors' land. I look forward to the communal dinners and love being in a house where brothers and sisters and uncles melt into one, sharing everything, down to their underwear. I admire their rejection of Western culture's nuclear family, how a day without Grandma, four aunts, eight cousins, and six uncles seems impossible.

And the boys! They flock at every stop in the road and wink as I enter and exit my father's store in central Dakar. The first time this happened, I believed the boys were approaching me because they wanted to know an American, a representative of this land of golden opportunities; celebrities on MTV; and beautiful, noncelibate women. But when they spoke to me in playful, flirtatious tones of Wolof, it dawned on me that these boys didn't know

I was from Brooklyn, USA. They were attracted to *me*. Me, the confidant who is always down to hear the details of her friends' conquests. Me, the tutor who gets attention from males only in exchange for help on English papers and biology projects. Me, the object who decorates Brooklyn parties and Dublin dances with my "new" kind of beauty that is "exotic" enough to praise but too African to touch.

Senegal allowed me to flirt without fear of rejection and just be in the moment. It's where, at sixteen, he kissed me. Where he stood over me and made my head spin and my insides flutter. In the most unexpected place, I had my first taste of lust and love all in one.

Senegal is where I feel *beautiful*.

He and Senegal are a 3,000-mile trek across the Atlantic. I hold on to the memories and plan to move across the ocean after I graduate from Spelman College. In the meantime, I continue to face the see-sawing emotions that come with colorism. On bad days, I salve my wounds with the whys. I remind myself of our horrific history and the slave psychology it created. Placed within this context, it hurts a little less when my friends brag about the Indian and Italian and Scottish blood they supposedly have in their veins but fail to mention their African lineage.

Then on good days, when the sun is shining, I have revelations. I am like the reddish-black sand of Kaolack. My skin is like the rich soil that nurtures the sugar cane on the island of Barbados, like the dirt of my uncle's garden where I plunge my toes. I am an African woman. Whether my skin is seared or lightly tanned, it represents Blackness. And that is a good thing.

Aminata Cisse, nineteen, is a sophomore at Spelman College in Atlanta, Georgia, majoring in anthropology.

FLESH IS BEST

Jill Nelson

Photo courtesy of Jill Nelson.

I'm a writer. I live most of the time in my head, in a world of words. What I love about my body is that words are not necessary to communicate with it. My body responds to visual stimuli, to touch and smell, to the feel of silk against bare skin, to my hands kneading lotion into flesh, to the smell of oils in a steaming bath. It whispers or shouts what it likes and what it doesn't. My body allows me to escape not only my mind but everyone else's, too.

I cannot recall a time when I have not been curious about my body and fascinated by its changes. I have always explored and touched it without shame. I remember the sensation of washing my genitals as a girl and feeling something surprising when my washcloth rubbed against my clitoris. Being amazed by the way my nipples became erect and sensitive when I soaped them in the shower. How, in the process of oiling my body, I'd graze a spot behind my knee or under my arm and feel aroused.

My parents raised me in a home where sexuality was neither denied nor condemned. Always on weekend mornings—and some other times, too—the door to their bedroom was locked and off-limits. Even before I had a clear idea of what my parents were doing in there, I knew it was a good thing. I could tell this by their smiles when they emerged, the signs of physical affection, the murmurs and chuckles that passed between them, the relaxation that emanated from my normally tense father, the fact that my mother made us French toast and bacon even though it was almost noon.

My mother was also there to provide answers for my most probing questions. She was a librarian and a great reader, and if you asked her a question she couldn't answer, within a few days she'd find a book that could. From the time I was a girl, my mother was straight up about sex and sexuality. I never believed that the stork brought babies, that you could get pregnant by kissing, that the key to happily-ever-after was keeping your skirt down and legs crossed. She gave me facts, with pictures and diagrams when appropriate.

By the time I became interested in boys, I had already unearthed my body's complexities through self-stimulation and after-school touching games with girlfriends. My breasts weren't simply things to fill a sweater, tease boys' eyes, or, in the distant future, nurse a baby. They were my soft, warm globes, pebbly around the aureole, a joy to touch. My stomach was not something to be held in, but a warm slope down to that place where I could elicit all measure of good feeling. So when I had my first sexual experiences, I was thrilled but not shocked by the warming between my legs when someone else's tongue explored my mouth or a boyfriend first touched my chest through several layers of clothing.

Yet as I moved into adolescence, puberty, and young womanhood, it was as if my body had two selves. One was the public body that had to be denied: constrained, covered, and kept in check so that I could move around without being catcalled and objectified. This was confusing, because it was the same tall, solid presence I'd wielded well in sports and used as a tool of intimidation in neighborhood squabbles.

The other was my private body—lush, loose, a self-affirming world in itself. That body was to be put under deep cover to emerge only when? When I was grown? When I got married? All that was clear was that there was no place for this private body in the public world. I saw women around me trapped in a negative narrative of its public nemesis: "You're too fat, you're too thin, learn to hold your stomach in! Say what you want and you're a ho', just let him do his thing and go! Your pussy smells like fish, go down on him 'cause that's his wish! Nice girls don't really like sex, now keep repeating this oppressive text!"

It seemed impossible to reconcile these two bodies, nor did I really want to. So as a teenager, I began the journey of saying to hell with the public body, the one suffocated by the values, judgments, expectations, and sometimes dangerous fantasies of others. I fought against being defined by my external physicality.

That I turned eighteen in 1970—a high point of the Women's Liberation Movement and five years after the widespread availability of the birth control pill—saved me. Among women, Black Americans, gays, Latinos, and workers, liberation—personal and political—defined the times. Burning bras and looking at our genitalia in the mirror may seem strange or passé today, but the message then was revolutionary. "Do your thing and know thyself!" were the rallying cries I heard and uttered as I stepped into womanhood. And the pill made our slogans a possibility, virtually vanquishing the fear of unwanted pregnancy. Finally, women were free to have sex just for fun.

As I became sexually active in my late teens, the act was more than a passing amusement. At its best sex is like wasabi, so intense that it clears the mind and washes away earthly concerns. Simply put, sex became my ultimate relaxation and high, and my body—not red rose romance or even soul-twisting love—is the vehicle that gets me there.

I have known a man who had a beautiful body with whom I would have sex for hours, after which he would read comic books and smoke herb as I drifted to sleep. I've known a man I called The Raptor, a wiry man able to wrap his body around mine in all kinds of ways who would not stop until even greedy me cried, "¡No más!" I have known a man with rather small hands who massaged my body so deftly that I reached orgasm just lying there. I have known a husky-voiced man thousands of miles away who could talk me to orgasm during late-night telephone calls. I have uncovered, explored, and honed my sexual character, tastes, and appetites with these men. I discovered not only how to give pleasure to another person, but accomplished the much more difficult work of knowing how to ask for and receive those things that pleasure me.

I've had men tell me, most often in a moment of annoyance or at a parting, that when it comes to sex, I think like a man. Even though they don't mean it as such, I consider this a compliment. What they mean is that I'm able to have sex solely for the physical joy of it, without the emotional attachment and drama that is commonly associated with women and sexual intercourse.

You know that old saying, men see sex as sex and women see sex as love? It's only true because of the blinders society puts on women's sexuality and the ways in which we facilitate those blinders. Because it's what's expected or because we're scared of who we might discover within ourselves if we took off that harness and let ourselves see—and feel—freely.

Imagine a world where women know their bodies; know what gives them pleasure; and feel comfortable exercising, stroking, and feeding their desire, with a partner or alone.

Imagine if we all knew that masturbation exists in a realm all its own, that it is not furtive or something to do when you don't have a partner. All alone I have learned that my body is my personal instrument, one that I should learn to play and use as a tool for pleasure, then, if I choose, to teach others how to play as well. Self-pleasuring with the help of a vibrator, other sex toys, or simply with my fingers has been the key to learning the instrument.

I'm not saying it's easy to overcome the oppressive conditionings we get from our books and newspapers, in our schools, in most religions, and embedded under various guises in popular culture. But I can testify that it's definitely worth the work. The alternative is to live our sexual lives defined by a sick, sexually obsessed, violent society; an oppressive patriarchy; and the expectations of a lot of people who aren't in our skin or beds but have the arrogance to tell us how we should behave in both.

NAKED

After a sex life that spans more than thirty years, what I know for sure is that learning the ways in which I can use my body as a tool of pleasure is an endless process; one that, like my body, is always changing. My weight goes up and down; my breasts are one size, then swell; my aureole change color and texture; my pubic hair thins; the smell between my legs, under my arms, of sweat generally, constantly mutates. I observe, take note, exercise, make adjustments, and eat right to keep this instrument in good shape, as finely tuned as possible. I think often and thankfully of the words of a long-ago lover who, when I asked him if I was too fat, gently held my shoulders, looked me in the eyes, and whispered, "Jill. Flesh is best. Don't forget it." I haven't.

Jill Nelson, fifty-two, is a journalist and author of three books of nonfiction. Her most recent book is the novel *Sexual Healing*.

THE FREE
BLACK WOMAN

Akiba Solomon

Photo by G. Giraldo.

Whenever Carmen Parker walks by, I study how the boys react. Mouth frothing, pupils Krazy Glued to her chest, one inevitably crows, "That's my *wife!*" to which another retorts, "Nah man, that's *my* wife!" Of course the biracial upperclasswoman doesn't belong to either boy. But her brand of 1989 flyness makes her ripe for claiming: Gucci sneakers and gold doorknocker earrings; pale-pink skin, hazel eyes, and a naturally blond, shoulder-length asymmetrical bob.

Word among some of the less remarkable Central High girls is that Carmen is "mixed up," "conceited," "dumb," and "a ho." As one of many "dark-skinned jawns" at our public magnet school, I, too, am entitled to indulge in this kind of jealous wound-licking. I abstain though. I've never even met the girl. Hating her on sight would be like playing in the one White girl's hair at day camp—covetous, self-loathing, and pathetic.

Besides, I can't believe—I *won't* believe—that Carmen's pale skin and long blonde hair are the main source of her sorcery. If that's the case, then a brown girl like me has no hope.

My resistance lasts until the day that Carmen and a male fan plop down at my lunch table.

"I just got a kitten," she tells him.

"For *real*? You got a kitten?" he says in a tone usually reserved for a five-year-old bearing macaroni jewelry and a dookie-shaped ashtray.

"Yes! I got a kitten, and he is soooo cute!!!"

"Wow. Did he get his shots yet?"

I wait for the punch line of the inane exchange but it never comes. I quit the cafeteria, stunned by the unfairness of it all. No brown girl I know could get away with prattling about her cat unless she was talking about the furry thing between her legs. We're living in an era of crack, cheap guns, gold-snatching, and beatdowns, but Carmen Parker gets to luxuriate in other-worldy silliness?

So I decide to hate her for this. I hate the boys who sweat her. I hate myself for comparing myself to another Black girl and for feeling so desperate for male attention. I was raised to be smarter than this.

I live on a quiet, working-class West Philly block where people mind their business. My parents, closet socialist Black Nationalists, filled my childhood with Black books, Black dolls, Black music, and Black love. At the Solomon home, the ultimate purpose of The Revolution (to improve peoples of color's standard of living) was discussed over dinner. Thanksgiving found us reading passages of a chapbook about "the one-eyed devil White Man" who spilled the blood and stole the gold of our African ancestors. Christmas didn't exist; it was all about Kwanzaa.

On an intellectual level, my parents' messages were pretty clear: Black is beautiful. Africa is the shit. Transatlantic slavery and Reconstruction are crimes against humanity. But things got screwy between third and eighth grade when my sister and I—affirmative action babies on partial scholarship— were bused out to Baldwin, a suburban, all-girls prep school that happened to be about 99 percent White.

In an attempt to clarify, my father once said that we were in this foreign land of lacrosse, Le Sportsacs, and "LikeohmyGod!" to obtain superior education that we'd use to administer The Revolution.

Remembering the time when I puffed out my cheeks Dizzy Gillespie–style for laughs, the time a White girl called me big lips and I failed to punch her in her thin kisser, his explanation terrified me. At twelve, I was already a counterrevolutionary Uncle Tom!

That was then. After spending four years among my people at Central High School, I believe I've escaped the confusion, loneliness, guilt, and self-hatred that I felt at Baldwin. I have a crew of girlfriends who don't seem to care about my suburban exile. I've moved house party crowds with my Cabbage

Patch and Running Man prowess, and I keep a fresh pair of Reeboks on my feet.

At fifteen, I had a popular Bobby Brown look-alike sweat me enough to garner a prank call from his girlfriend. At sixteen, I foisted my cursed virginity on a graffiti-writing Five Percenter who moved back to Cali before he could tell anybody that he was the first boy I ever kissed.

And now, at seventeen, I'm ready for the ultimate—to be claimed by an "intelligent hoodlum." For me, success with a street-smart but well-read, sweet but dangerous, sexually experienced but selective cross between Malcolm X and Big Daddy Kane would prove that I wasn't inferior or White-acting or weird or unreal. Pulling an intelligent hoodlum would earn me full citizenship to urban, Black America.

Now in my approximation, there are two kinds of girls who get the intelligent hoodlums I want. In first place float the light, bright princesses like Carmen Parker. Treading in distant second are the pedestrian-but-cute Regular Black Girls who have been doing it since they were thirteen. In lieu of "good hair" and "pretty eyes," Regular Black Girls are thoroughbreds—enterprising, tart-tongued, quick-witted, and "down to the gristle." Most seem to be the same color brown I am, so that's what I'll have to be.

So I weigh the pros and cons of Akiba. Pro: I'm bow-legged. Con: I'm wired to be the Irregular Black Girl. Pro: I have a fat butt. Con: I'm not light-skinned with long hair, so there aren't any boys trying to rescue my Black ass from the margins.

Despite the crazy-making colorism I've internalized, I know that I am not ugly. In fact, Caribbean, Muslim, and Five Percent boys have told me that

I am so gorgeous that I must be Jamaican, Ethiopian, or something more exotic than what I am: the descendent of Down South Negroes. Others get right to the point: I am "pretty for a dark-skinned girl." It's not that these dudes are colorstruck. It's just difficult, they say, to find an attractive, intelligent, classy African American female like me. That is supposed to make me proud.

It doesn't.

In theory, I know that no complexion is better than another. But reality tells me things like, "Lightness would give you more power and options," and "If you were light, you could be Afrocentric by choice instead of necessity."

Then there's that thing that happened when I saw *School Daze*, Spike Lee's musical about colorism at historically Black colleges. I envied the high yella, mean-spirited but sexy "wannabes" and wished the multihued "jiggaboos" would just get perms and shut the fuck up.

Plus there's that interesting, secret thing involving Ambi and my face. I intended to fade an acne scar the size of a raw sugar grain. But the circumference of the black spot wouldn't stop growing. Two months into my quest for beautiful, even-toned skin, my sister, Asali, asked me why my face looked so light. I played dumb and tossed out my tube of equalizer the next time I had a private moment.

And there was that incident when I was six and Asali was seven. Someone gave us these vintage baby dolls. One was charcoal gray with a short 'fro. To me she looked like a boy. The other was café au lait and had a bouncy, girly bob. Before I could throw a tantrum for the pretty baby, my sister chose the ugly charcoal one and named her Carolyn after our paternal grandmother who died before we were born. If I had known the word *integrity*, I would have been able to express what I lacked at that moment.

At seventeen, I know how to conceal my conflict. The Black Nationalist orthodoxy of the Solomon family may make me an inner sinner, but on the surface I look the part. My hair has been natural since that day in late 1990 when I got more play in the 'hood with a kinky-looking wet-set than I ever did rocking a permed asymmetrical bouffant. I have traded my summer-job gold for my mom's silver bangles. Sometimes I rock geles like the giant yellow one Aretha wore on the cover of *Young, Gifted and Black*.

My parents think that I've fallen in step with their liberation march, but I'm receiving most of my cues from the Golden Age flurry of pro-Black hip-hop artists such as Public Enemy, KRS-One, and De La Soul. They, along with Spike Lee's marketing of Malcolm X paraphernalia, have made my upbringing feel relevant. For the first time in my life, I am in style.

Most importantly, I'm attracting a new crop of prospects. No more soft-suckers with corny gear, high butts, and jagged fades. Now I attract college men and fledgling rap artists. Fine-ass activists over twenty-five. Grimy out-of-towners crashing the same college parties my sister and I do.

Between proms, college visits, and Greek picnics, I do worry about the inevitable backlash. I predict that by the time I'm nineteen, I will again be one shade shy of invisible. So while I have access to a decent pool of suitors, I'll need to develop a certain skill.

*   *   *

Which brings me to the man standing over me. He doesn't know about my aspirations of superfreakdom. That I need him to laud my good pussy and supreme head instead of my sweetness and cultural awareness. I don't care that this twenty-one-year-old Temple University junior with the Bronx growl and weed-stained lips says I'm smart. I think he's dumb. And trifling. And so fine that I am afraid of him.

Despite his shortcomings, I have fallen in love with what he represents. I love his butterscotch Timberland boots in the summer, his beat-making and counterfeit-money printing. He is a second-generation Jamaican American who grew up middle class, but he still seems to have street cred. He is a spoiled fuck-up who never takes me anywhere.

At first I believe that he sequesters me in his bedroom because I bore him. Our telephone conversations are awkward because he is too high to discuss Frantz Fanon, BDP, and Donny Hathaway.

So we sit, often in silence, until he asks me when I plan to board the el, transfer to the sub, and walk over two blocks to his one-bedroom where I will swallow him without as much as a Happy Meal.

About three months into this compromising ritual, I enter his walk-in closet and find a framed studio photo of him and a girl.

She has slanted eyes and nearly translucent light skin. Her hair is too wispy to hold a hot curl. Her breasts challenge the front flank of her Polo shirt. Played-out gold doorknockers abuse her earlobes.

And him! His arms are wrapped around her like vines. Tentacles. The hard chocolate coating of a vanilla Dairy Queen dip cone. He is proud enough to be seen with her to pose for a Sears photographer. I am the opposite of her. Therefore, he must think that I deserve equally opposing treatment.

So our talk goes something like this:

Me: "Who is that?"

Him: "What are you talking about?"

Me: "Who the fuck is that girl in the picture?"

Him [*smirking*]: "Who you cussing at? You have such a dirty mouth to be such a young girl."

Me: "Just answer the motherfuckin' question!"

Him [*chuckling*]: "Yo, you don't even sound right saying that. I don't wanna fight. Come here. Don't be mad."

I cry. He tells me she's just his ex. I'm still crying. He rolls a blunt and I, a nonsmoker, take long pulls. He gets up to pee. While he's in the bathroom, I undress myself and, in a dramatic flourish, I cross my arms across my chest like a corpse. I want him to see my desperation, but when he returns he already has on a condom. He pulls me on top of him and commands me to "move that big ass, girl."

He doesn't kiss me afterward, but it doesn't matter. My mouth feels like that white fuzzy cash crop my ancestors picked back in Roanoke Rapids, North Carolina.

Before I leave for Florida A&M University, where I have a full academic scholarship, my "love" says he'll write. About a month after I arrive in Tallahassee,

I receive his letter. A photo and a few paragraphs about what a good fuck I've become. It's a demeaning victory.

I don't respond. I've replaced him with a dark-skinned upperclassman from Brooklyn who has seduced me with a hard-luck story, a Ron G. mixtape, and a tepid bowl of spaghetti.

The first couple of nights I spend at his apartment he gives me the bed and takes the floor. At my request, he makes a framed photo of his high school sweetheart, a café au lait cheerleader type with waist-length, wavy hair, disappear.

Before ten days have passed, I am horny, homesick, and tired of "playing coy." I ask him if we, two "mature adults," have a strong enough friendship to sustain sex. He says yes.

Two days later I find out that I am a 'ho. Word around campus is that I have not only fucked (true) and sucked (false) him, but I've given up the ass to two of his boys. If these clowns down here knew literary references, they would call me the Black Hester Prynne. Instead they opt for, "Yeah, I hit that, too, son!"

Back home for Thanksgiving, I spend the night with the chocolate drop from the summer. I haven't let on that I am a very different, very traumatized girl. Misplacing my trust has earned me the label of whore. And I have become a magnet for hostility. Walking back to the dorm from a party, my friends and I were cornered by a Jeep full of drunken football player types who uttered menacing nonsequitirs like, "Why y'all actin' all scared like we gonna rape y'all? Maybe we *should* rape y'all . . ." Another time, a five-foot asshole from Jacksonville pushed me into the cafeteria conveyer belt because I rejected his advances. As I cursed him out, his homeboys formed a human chain around us to ask him if he was OK. And for "talking too fuckin' much," another Jacksonvillan threatened to beat me with the metal buckle of a cowboy belt. My assailants were weak misogynists, but I blame myself.

I keep sucking.

It's second semester in Tallahassee. I'm lying on a motel bed next to a drug-selling Five Percenter. He lives down here because he was firebombed out of Brooklyn.

Since meeting him at the one mall in this town, I've had to rethink my opposition to gold teeth and Tec-9s. He has both.

Yet somehow I feel safe. College boys put light-skinned ex-girlfriends in golden picture frames but treat dark-skinned girls like common, broke bitches. Hardrock dudes give you piggyback rides to the ice machine and assure you that if anyone busts into the room, they'll "whet 'em up." I could love this man, I think.

During the ride back to my dorm he asks me to pay his electric bill. I decline but miss him anyway.

It's June 1993, summer in Philly again. So far I've had a little situation with shoplifting and a holding cell. My favorite uncle pays the fine.

My mom asks me why I'm acting so strange. I don't share any details. If she knew what I was up to, she'd derail my plan to rekindle the relationship I had with this Rasta back in high school. He has since shorn his dreds, trashed his mesh tank tops, and started selling crack. My intellect and political consciousness disapprove of his poisonous hustle. My emotional self wants to be down.

See, in the same niche of my brain where I've tucked the shame of the Baldwin and Ambi incidents, I've stashed the lyrics of "Gangsta Bitch." This 1992 rap anthem by a one-hit wonder named Apache identifies and celebrates the archetype of the sexy, powerful, ghetto antiheroine. The video stars Nikki D, a thick, dark-skinned rapper who is Apache's real-life love. "Gangsta Bitch" makes real my fantasy of the Regular Black Girl.

I suppose that explains why I accompany my nickel-and-dime knucklehead to his workplace, a remote cul-de-sac blanketed with broken glass, chicken bones, and Katankelon extensions. As he runs up to hoopties full of White customers, I chat with two dark-skinned Regular Black Girls whom I am sure have been doing it since they were thirteen.

Weave tracks askew, postpregnancy bellies pushing dollar-store seams, they look a hot mess. They have to be pushing thirty, but their angel dust highs have them fiending for some Double Dutch. Before I can join my sisters in this childhood rite of Regular Black Girls, my boyfriend summons me. "Are you nuts?" he asks me. "You don't know these crazy bitches. I think it's time to go."

During a subsequent late-night telephone conversation, he tells me about the time he murdered someone. The next morning I decide that my mother is right. I do need some therapy.

* * *

By July, I'm meeting regularly with a middle-aged Afrocentric psychologist who asks me why I am trying to become a "street rat." I realize that no matter how cryptic I am about what I've been doing, my goal is transparent and ridiculous. For about a year, I've been giving my body to certified hoodlums, thinking that they would legitimize me, yet I feel more abnormal, ashamed, and weak than I did when I started. I decide to abort my mission.

About a month into my self-imposed celibacy, I start falling in love with a blue-black rapper with a Muslim name. He's been trying to talk to me since we met last summer, but I rejected him because his Jesus sandals seemed so soft.

Now that I feel like a piece of sun-dried dog dirt, I need someone to sweat me. He doesn't do that. Instead, he actually takes me out on dates. We see films with subtitles and take walks on Penn's Landing. He writes a poem about the depth of my chocolate kiss. He also refuses sex. Intercourse cheapens things, he says.

We hold out until October when he visits me in Washington, D.C., at my new university, Howard. I haven't gotten the proper clearance for him to stay at my dorm, so we make love on the back steps of the student center. And we fall asleep.

Through this man, this Libra poet, I finally made sense of my beautiful African self. He had no light-skinned princesses tucked away in his closet.

He praised the angry poetry I started writing about ex-boyfriends and prep school scars. "Take out your braids," he pleaded. "Grow dreds."

Then he got a record contract and a pistol. He started smoking lots of weed and bringing strangeness into our bed. We fight too much, and he leaves me, snatching back the sense of self I believed I'd actually earned.

So now it's September 1994, and I'm back at Howard. Despite my continuing therapy and plans to procure some Prozac, I am too depressed to function. I miss lots of sleep, skip many meals, and shed mad pounds.

One day, I take an entire bottle of Nuprin. I'm not quite ready to die, so I vomit up bitter, yellow slime and tell Akiba how much I hate her for being too soft to do the damn thing.

Now I'm perched on the window ledge of my eleventh-floor apartment. Now my parents are here. I can't recall how to form sentences.

In a Philly-area hospital, I believe that I am a slave. I think the orderlies who tackle me when I try to escape are CIA agents. The TV is telling me that I'm an ugly, crispy, crackhead-looking thing.

My Jewish on-site psychiatrist asks my parents why I seem to hate White people so much. If I could form the words, I'd say it's because they won't let me go home.

Severe clinical depression with a psychotic episode. That's my diagnosis. Now that I'm out of the hospital with meds coursing through my system, I can look in the mirror without bugging out. I can see why my sister kept excusing herself during her visit.

Although my normal weight is about 130 pounds, I'm barely making 105. My hair, once a focus of my vanity, is Brillo-pad dry. My eyes gape as if I'm imitating Mantan Moreland, a minister of minstrelsy.

Yet at my ugliest, I feel new. I don't have to be a Regular Black Girl. No matter whom I fuck, have sex with, or make love to, I will never be normal. I have the discharge papers to prove it. I am certifiably crazy!

The euphoria of my rebirth has dissipated. Now I have to relearn how to do things like take the bus without having a panic attack. That's how I'm going to spend this semester off from Howard.

I busy myself with nurturing things. I audit an African American history course and go to Rites of Passage. I write and sing songs, read trashy fiction, and go dancing. I've taken to wearing lipstick again—a cinnamon brown. My hair, now a short Caesar, earns me compliments from both men and women who don't know enough of my business to pity me.

One day, as I'm coming home from a therapy appointment, two little chestnut girls stop dead in front of me and chant, "She's pretty! She's pretty! She's pretty!" Their mother, with a mixture of mortification and pride, tells me that she's been showing her daughters a calendar of "beautiful African princesses" and that I resemble a woman in one of the pictures. I thank them for making me smile, and I tell them that they're gorgeous, too.

Once they're at the opposite end of the train platform, I take out a hand mirror. I can barely see the signs of pretty that compelled those children to stop, but I do know that they are there. I just have to retrain my eyes to recognize them without external cues.

It is 2005. I'm thirty. I stand upright, some days on my tip-toes. I know who I am, outside of the conflicting political and social realities that shaped my beautiful mind.

Here's one of the great things about getting grown: you learn that you've been duped. I spent much of my adolescence and young adulthood punishing myself for not being born and raised the proverbial Regular Black Girl. I tried to use my body and sexuality to become her. It might have worked if the Regular Black Girl were an actual human being. But she doesn't exist. She is a toxic cocktail of White supremacist, misogynist stereotypes—Sapphire with a Jezebel chaser.

Because I was raised to critique colorism, racism, and messages of Black inferiority, I believed that I was immune to pain. When I found out that I wasn't, I felt like a weak, repulsive traitor.

Outside of my family home, among my peers, I was desperate for nurturing, nuanced messages about Black womanhood, power, and sexuality. Slogans like, "Protect and respect the Black woman" didn't count; they were still about the male role. Those at the opposite end of the spectrum such as, "All men are dogs" and "Fuck niggas, get money" were downright dangerous, as they were grounded in dehumanizing stereotypes—Black male as stud, Black female as concubine.

After literally losing my mind and misusing my body, I've learned the importance of defining myself and coming up with my own messages.

I am a free Black woman. It's a descriptive phrase, not a titular albatross. With "free Black woman," I am officially reclaiming the sensitivity, sweetness, and even the silliness I once envied Carmen Parker for expressing.

I give "free Black woman" to sisters of all hues. If I could, I'd press it into the hands of every young girl out there who calls herself a "down-ass bitch," a "ghetto princess," a "project chick," or whatever else our concrete troubadours serve up.

I want us all to call ourselves free Black women and to work toward a day when it's actually true.

Akiba Solomon is a co-editor of *Naked* and the health editor at *Essence* magazine.

SELLING SEXUALITY

Kelis

As told to Margeaux Watson

Photo by Markus Klinko.

This is not a new phenomenon. From Josephine Baker to Billie Holiday, Marilyn Monroe to Lena Horne, women throughout history have played on and exploited their sensuality and beauty, using their talent as their second-best feature.

The reality is that this is what I have, this is what I look like, and if it is going to get me a little closer to where I need to be, fine. Men don't have to be sexy and beautiful; they have different avenues to take to success. I am really smart, and really talented, but when I started out in the music industry, I learned right away that it's not enough to just look cute and stylish. I could have done it, but it would have been much harder. Sex sells. It's sad, but true.

It's not just hip-hop. And it's bigger than Black music. *America* is all about what is appealing to the eye. And I have a better chance of getting where I want looking the way I do than trying to be a burlap-wearing, waving-incense-wherever-I-go woman. God bless those who go that route, but it's not for me. One day I'll be older and not quite as cute, with tits not as perky and an ass not as round. But right now? I'll be damned if I'm going to hide what God gave me.

I hate when women say that being female is a curse. That's only true if you want it to be. My body is a gift. So if you believe that having a pussy and tits stifles rather than propels you, that's your brain making it a reality, not your tits. I know that men don't have to deal with this, but life's not fair. No one ever promised you fair.

Kelis is an internationally acclaimed recording artist. Her latest album, her third, is titled *Tasty*.

LA NERA

Ayana Mathis

"Hey big legs," "Hey, where y'all goin'? Can I come?" The young Black men standing on the corners near my friend Sasha's house were a fixture in her Philadelphia neighborhood. We were sixteen, with better things to think about than the guys on the corner, and so we usually just ignored them. But that day, Sasha turned around and yelled "Fuck you! Leave us alone!" She ground out her cigarette with a stomp and lit another one right afterward. "I'm just sick of them. I have to hear this shit everyday. You know, when White men say stuff to me on the street, it's nice, like a compliment. When Black men do it, it just feels dirty." Despite my wholehearted agreement, my inner voice whispered that there was something wrong with what she'd said. I couldn't explain my feelings and so I just pulled hard on my cigarette and said nothing.

I was only a teenager, had never had a boyfriend, but I had already learned that the body and sexuality were commodities, bartering tools to be exchanged for love, acceptance, and popularity. And I was sure that I had come to the table with an inferior product. I was poor, Black, and fat (*big-boned* was my family's polite term for it), and believed that the bulky reality of my physical self made me unlovable. As I saw it, only Black men like the ones who had just called out to us were interested. Black men liked the parts of me that I hated, thick thighs and legs, a Black woman's thighs and legs. How could they like those ugly, shamefully large parts of my body? I decided it was because only someone who has no choice would choose what no one else wants.

White boys were different. They were sons of men who went to work in suits every morning, of men who ran the banks and taught at universities. They were the offspring of parents who gave them cars and would one day pay for college. White boys were safe and secure.

On television, in the media, in the world swirling around me, we seemed always to have less—less respect, less opportunity, less money. Everywhere I looked, Black people were in the same boat that I was, buffeted and battered by forces that I couldn't yet name. I knew that there was something terribly wrong. The problem was that I blamed Black people.

I was a teenager during the Reagan era, with its images of poor Black women, fat and despised, their lives metered out in public assistance checks and food stamps, the Welfare Queen. Sitting around in curlers all day, her situation made even more desperate by the fact that she just kept having babies. Instead of getting a job, the media told us, or even a high school diploma, she just fucked all the time, a grotesque oversexed whore, unable to control her raging libido.

Talk of welfare reform was everywhere, debates in Congress, in the news-papers, in living rooms all over America. I remember the matriarch of one family, featured on a news special: a grossly obese woman with long, bright-red nails and her hair pinched back into a ponytail from which broken strands stuck out at wild angles. Sitting on a park bench holding forth about how few food stamps she received every month, the waddle on her arms flapped as she waved and swatted at the children scampering in and out of the camera's eye. I looked down at my own body and was deeply and violently ashamed. I saw myself in her, the same brown skin, the same wide fleshy hips, the same ample breasts. I wanted to distance myself from her and everything she represented. I considered myself intelligent, capable, and yes, even lovable, but all of those qualities were hidden away in the hateful Welfare Queen's body. How different everything would be, I used to think, if only I were a pretty and little White girl.

Instead, I dealt with the cumbersome bulk by covering it up. From thirteen to nineteen I wore only voluminous sweaters, massive T-shirts, and baggy jeans. Above all, never skirts. I had decided somewhere along the line that if I weren't a thin White girl, I somehow wasn't a girl at all. At seventeen I wrote this poem:

> *I was never meant to shine.*
> *I will not glide in sequined black,*
> *Sparkling in the moonlight.*
> *I am anonymous as burlap.*
> *My femininity—*
> *No more than a whisper*
> *Echoing in an empty room.*

During my senior year in high school, through mutual friends at one of our favorite afterschool hangouts, I met Daniel. About a month into our relationship, we arranged to spend the night together at a friend Peter's house when his parents were away for the weekend.

My palms were sweaty. When we opened the door to Peter's bedroom, all I could think was how bright the overhead light was and how he would see everything, the big hips, the large behind, the whole bulk of me. I fought back shame as we fumbled on the bed. He said he liked my breasts and touched them, making methodical little circles around the nipples. When I thought he was too caught up in the moment to notice, I turned off the light and we slipped under the covers. I hoped he wouldn't touch my hair, straightened into a limp brownish sheet and pulled into a tight ponytail. Not at all like his White ex-girlfriend's pretty long brown hair. He kissed my neck, bit my ear-lobes, reached down and unzipped my jeans. His breath came in short bursts, exploding in my ears, and I felt some fleeting physical pleasure, a sweet ache and I almost forgot that my thighs were huge and horrible. I hoped that maybe he did, too. I moaned when I thought I should, touched him where I knew he wanted me to, arched my back, and cried out when it seemed the right time. Then it was over, and we lay there talking and smoking cigarettes and all I could think was, *I have a boyfriend and we've had sex and I'm real now, I exist.*

My boyfriend, it even sounded odd saying it, but I did say it, often and to everyone. And Daniel was not just any boy; he was a boy who lived in a huge house in one of the exclusive quarters of Germantown. A boy who went to an expensive private school, a boy who drove a Saab and brought me to his house to eat dinner with his very wealthy, very White family. I loved him desperately.

It wasn't the money. I didn't want anything material from him. It was what he represented that I was after.

Daniel picked me up after school in the Saab, and we had sex in his bedroom before his parents came home. I wrote poems about him, dreamt about him. I skipped school and wandered the city, listening to Sade on my headset and thinking about him. I relived the scene in Peter's bedroom a thousand times and thought about when I'd see him next.

Sex, I discovered, was liberating. It was so simple. I gave pleasure, played the wild, uninhibited lover in exchange for feeling desired and worthy, if only for a few hours. After one of our marathon make-out sessions in the back of his car, Daniel told me that I gave the best blow job he'd ever had. I was so proud. I stopped myself from wondering if somewhere in the back of his mind he thought, even just once, *It's true what they say about Black girls.* Instead, I faked wild orgasms with theatrical passion, determined to prove my value with sex.

Terry played basketball at the court on West 4th Street. It was the summer of 1992, and I had a tiny apartment in Manhattan's East Village and a job in a coffee shop. He was a huge light-brown-skinned man, almost 6' 5", and when we walked the streets with his arm around me, I felt small and precious. We'd have sex on my loft bed, his hands holding onto the thighs that I still hated. Terry never let me turn off the lights or hide under the covers. He wanted to see me. He said I looked amazing, my skin was beautiful, my body was round and sexy like a woman's body is supposed to be, and he wanted to see it.

I discovered my body with Terry. Or rather, he discovered it for me. I used to wrap myself in a sheet anytime I had to leave the bedroom and he'd wait for me by the door and rip away the blanket, exposing me to the gaze of the overhead lamp and the mirror resting against the opposite wall. He held me there once, running his hands over my entire body as he stood behind me. The breasts, big but firm; the thighs, not as horrible as I'd thought; the stomach, surprisingly flat!; and big, strong legs. *It's not so awful*, I thought. *Maybe there's even something just a little beautiful about the way the bones of my clavicle reach toward one another or the smooth, brown skin of my stomach, just a shade darker than Terry's fingers tracing little circles around my belly button.* That night, at twenty years old, I saw my naked body for the first time.

Literature continued the process that Terry had begun. Sonia Sanchez, Toni Morrison, Lucille Clifton, and a host of other Black female writers gave me a new mirror in which to find my image. They dethroned the Welfare Queen and replaced her with poems and novels in which Black women were actually *women*, not caricatures or cruel stereotypes. I studied African and African American culture and politics. It was like scar tissue falling away to reveal an angry red wound underneath. The politics of race and gender had come to the forefront of my life. I felt duped, cheated, wrestled to the ground by forces that I had not even known existed, even as I struggled under their weight.

Walking home from work late one night, a group of drunken White guys called out, "Hey brown sugar, why don't you come over here." They were dressed in T-shirts with the names of rock bands written across the chest and khaki shorts—the same White guys I had gone to high school with, the same ones I had been friends with for all those years. I was stunned into silence. The words were violent, violating, like an unwanted hand on my ass or arms pinning me down so that I couldn't move. I thought of the thousand things I could have said in response, and then thought that it wouldn't have made any difference. They wouldn't have understood anyway because they didn't have to. They could live their lives without ever giving a second thought to race or gender. *What did they see*, I wondered. Just brown hips, an ass, and tits. Maybe they'd heard their fathers use that phrase, maybe they remembered hearing them say that Black women were good for a fuck.

Later that night, sitting in my apartment, I cried for hours. I thought of some of my theatrics in high school with Daniel, the blow jobs that he talked about so enthusiastically. I felt like I had played right into the "hot jungle woman" stereotype that had been thrown in my face that evening. I thought about plantations and Black women being raped by White men, my own great-grandmother being raped. "Hey, brown sugar."

I dated only Black men from then on. The realities of being a Black woman in America, and the racial politics that go with them, just seemed too complicated for interracial relationships. I maintained friendships with White men but never allowed them to become sexual. I wondered how many White men, even the most intelligent and best informed of them, carried images of the supersexed Black woman somewhere in their psyches. I didn't want to be a White man's sexual rite of passage. And so I steered clear of them. It wasn't difficult. The sense of racial awareness and empowerment that I gained had profoundly changed my ideas of who and what was attractive. I didn't need White men anymore, and so I decided not to want them, either.

I still needed sex, though—having lovers gave me confidence. And in my relationships with Black men I found plenty to be confident about. Black men liked my big legs and round hips, and that appreciation was expressed so unabashedly that I could not help but follow suit. I dared to think that I could be attractive, pretty even, with a little effort. I discovered exercise, and my body seemed to me a kind of marvel. It could run five miles without stopping. It could bend into half moons in yoga class. I wore skirts and sleeveless shirts to show off long, lean arms. In the summer, I'd lie in the sun and wear white to accentuate the reddish undertone that appeared as my skin turned a deep chocolate brown, remembering days as a teenager when I had crossed to the shady side of the street for fear of getting darker.

As I grew to accept my body, I also let go of race-based shame and judgments, and I began to realize that I wanted more from relationships. Sex had lost its power to legitimize and validate, or rather I didn't need it to perform that function any longer. I looked back on the men who had been my lovers and admitted that sex had been the most important part of our relationships. The men were in many ways dispensable, there to help me prove to myself that I was desirable. I finally liked myself, Blackness and hips and kinky hair and all. Now I was alone, dissatisfied, and extraordinarily lonely.

"Europe is no different. You're kidding yourself if you think he's not just after some jungle booty." That was an ex-boyfriend's reaction to the blonde-haired, blue-eyed Italian I'd met while on vacation. He had shown me Italy, and we'd made love in his apartment and friends' bedrooms and beaches from Naples to Florence. We had no language, just my rusty Spanish and his broken English, so it was an affair of few words. An affair of gestures and gazes and a kind of intimacy that I could not remember having ever experienced.

But it didn't matter, his being White. In Italy it really hadn't mattered. In fact, it somehow seemed irrelevant. Race is lived differently in Italy. Immigration and otherness are a new phenomenon there. It is, of course, impossible to deny the presence of racial stereotypes or predjudices; they seem to exist in every corner of the earth. The crucial difference is that racial opinions are informed by curiosity and the occasional ignorance of a few, not by four centuries of systematic oppression.

I moved to Florence four months after that first visit. My passionate affair turned out to be nothing more than a travel romance, but by the time it ended I had fallen in love with Italy and decided to stay.

La nera. Translated it means, simply, "the Black girl." People who didn't even know my name knew *la nera.* I achieved a kind of fame in my first year in Florence, small city that it is. I was different, American, and Black. People noticed me on the street, remembered me. I was sought after, pursued by men who saw me as a novelty. But to be honest, I liked being different. In Italy, difference didn't mean shame or inferiority. It seemed to bring only good things. Popularity, friends, and, yes, lovers.

Lovers with lyrical names like Cesare and Davide. Lovers with whom I sat in the outdoor gallery of the Uffizi or watched the stars from a deserted Ponte Vecchio in the wee hours of the morning. In this new place, I was reborn. It wasn't so important why men wanted me, but why I wanted them. Because I liked them—what a relief! I liked them and they liked me and that was all. No great search for acceptance or normality. Nothing to prove. Sex because I enjoy it. Sex because it's an expression of passion, a kind of physical language, my body—with its thighs a little too robust, and those same ten pounds I've wanted to lose for years—an instrument.

"Do you ever think about it, that I'm Black and you're White?" We're lying in bed on a Sunday morning and looking down at our naked bodies, his pale leg thrown over my brown one; the contrast strikes me. "No," he answers, "do you?"

We've been together for nearly three years now. I don't question his motives, and I don't question mine. I've asked myself if I am still using my body and sexuality subconsciously playing out race issues, to gain acceptance in the arms of someone White. But then I think of all that led me to this place, this city, the home that I share with this man. It was a journey of rebirth through suffering, of knowledge gained through pain. And I realize that I'm not playing out anything. I'm just in love.

Ayana Mathis is a poet from Philadelphia who resides in Florence, Italy.

THE CURL

April Yvonne Garrett

Photo by Roy Cox.

I took Jojo's interest in me as a residual effect of The Curl. It had taken me a long time to grow some hair, and even though it was dripping all over the place, it was mine. As far as I was concerned, I had earned his crush.

Ronald Reagan, crack cocaine, and leggings were some of the obvious problems of the 1980s. Some folks might add the Jheri Curl to that list, but for me it was a blessing.

Jojo's mother, Ms. Anita, gave me The Curl. My mom had heard that it would grow my hair, a short, traumatizing natural that got me mistaken for a boy all too often. So after a day in the kitchen-cum-salon of her Baltimore row house, I was reborn. In the better part of an afternoon, I went from an unfashionably short-haired thirteen-year-old to someone glamorously hip like Michael Jackson. By my next appointment a few weeks later, Ms. Anita's younger son had noticed me. Before Jojo it had never occurred to me that anyone—male, female, child, or adult—might consider me cute. My family never put me down about how I looked, but my long-haired big sister and wavy-haired, half–Puerto Rican cousins were doted over nonstop. The Jheri Curl did a lot for equalizing things.

That was, of course, before The Tragedy. Weeks after my first kiss, an awkward peck that Jojo and I snuck behind a neighborhood church, I was sitting at Ms. Anita's getting a new Curl. Jojo and his brother were riding me for liking Duran Duran better than New Edition when they were silenced by the news flash: "Michael Jackson has been taken to the hospital for burns to the scalp after his hair caught fire during the filming of a Pepsi commercial. Story at 11." I burst into tears, glad that the boys both had Curls so they couldn't tease me unless they wanted to mock themselves. Regardless, I was still crushed. Here I had finally begun to feel some kind of social validation via my hairstyle, and now the world's biggest star was in the hospital because it was so dangerously flammable. By the time my mom came to pick me up I was hysterical.

Still, I held on to The Curl.

There were other problems. I regularly bathed pillowcases in Carefree Curl activator. Freshmen year in high school I had a huge crush on Dimitris, a Greek German soccer player who was one of the most popular guys in my class. I craved his attention, and one day, much to my surprise, he dropped by my locker to flirt. It was all going great, until he decided to give me a noogie. Before I could protest, Jheri Curl juice had smeared all over the front of his

Adidas jacket. I was mortified. He was confused, not totally sure what greasy substance was covering his jacket or, more importantly, if it would ever come out. I apologized profusely and scurried away. I thought he was the biggest gentleman ever when he never mentioned it to anyone.

After some trial and error and a fair amount of time studying beauty store shelves, I learned the critical difference between "moist" and "drippy." Because there's nothing worse than a dry Curl, I had been doing the extra juicy thing with the squirty stuff in the spray bottle. The activator gel, which wasn't quite so wet, saved my beloved Curl.

I couldn't fix the evil backlash, though. The Jheri Curl had saved a lot of Black people whose hair wouldn't grow and then, as a race, we turned on it. Those of us who stuck with the style really went through it. The fact that I was so popular at my predominantly Black high school in spite of my way-past-fashionable Curl says a lot about my tenacity.

There was a palpable, usually unspoken class issue going on among Black people, this stereotype that you must be ignorant, poor, and country if you wore a curl. It ran rampant through movies such as *Hollywood Shuffle*, *School Daze*, and *Coming to America*, and TV shows like *In Living Color*. Luckily, I always had considerate friends who spared me even the most "harmless" of teasing. The only disparaging comment I remember is when a classmate asked me, "Are you really going to wear that curl for prom?" Hell yeah. What did she think I was going to do?

By high school graduation in 1988, it had been more than four years since my first trip to Ms. Anita's chair. At this point, I realized that the style was more utilitarian than fashionable. But I couldn't think of a way out. Constricted by the cardinal rule of The Curl—you cannot transition into a re-laxer because the chemicals do not compliment one another—when most people grow out a Curl, they go for a short natural. That was not an option. I was too tender about my childhood as the "skinny baldheaded" Black girl to go back.

As a young child I'd have violent tantrums whenever my mother would leave me with a sitter. I'd bang my head on the floor and literally rip out my hair. To camouflage the unevenness, my mother cut my hair into natural that couldn't have been more than two inches high. It was practical, but this was Baltimore in the '70s and early '80s, a place and time when couplets such as "Becky Baldhead" and "nappy-ass" peppered schoolyard conversation. From teachers thinking I was "slow" because they equated "less attractive" with "less intelligent," to my older sister having to fight kids who teased her about her little "brother," I knew firsthand the prejudices held about short, natural hair.

So as the 1980s crept to an end, I was stuck with The Curl. I had asymmetrical bobs, neat chignons—all types of non-Jheri-specific styles that I adapted to my activator-dependant, shoulder-length mane. A few months after graduation, I packed up my Jheri Curl juice and headed off to Kenyon College in rural Ohio, where there wasn't a Black hairdresser for miles. When I ran through the bottles, my mother shipped reinforcements. There were also very few Black people, so my Curl and I were generally left alone—my White friends on campus were clueless about Black hair care.

While my hair stayed the same throughout college, I was changing. I was going through a political awakening, reading a lot of bell hooks, protesting the first Iraq war and apartheid, and being exposed to ideas from people like Maulana Karenga. Growing out The Curl was a part of that transformation. I just needed to figure out how to do it without lopping off my hair.

The summer after junior year I went back to Baltimore and kept seeing women with braids and cornrows, long, thin, and beautiful. When I was a little girl, my mom once made a derogatory remark about dredlocks. Even though her exact words escape me, I took her attitude about the style and extended it to braids, which I mistakenly thought were the same thing. Without really consciously considering why, I'd been wary of the style my whole life. But I really liked what I was seeing that summer. I had some trepidation about people stereotyping me as a militant or attaching me to the other radical ideas that Blacks and Whites attach to natural hair, but I decided to do it.

Five packs of hair and ten hours later, I had a numb head full of what looked like thousands of microbraids. I was floored by their beauty. After all those years with The Curl, it felt like a crossing over. And the braids seemed a lot more compatible to the Black feminist ultra-political rhetoric coming out of my mouth than my played-out Curl.

Braids took me from Kenyon to New York City to Atlanta to, finally, Boston. For the four years I wore them, I didn't feel stereotyped because of my choice in hairstyle. It wasn't until I replaced them—at first with a permed, Halle Berry pixie and later with an add-on ponytail followed by a mid-back-length weave—that people assumed they knew me just by how I wore my hair.

You can have braid extensions down to your knees and people will still be like, "Black power, sister." You get a weave to your shoulders, and those same folks will accuse you of wanting to be White. First of all, I know braids are culturally based, but both styles require hair extensions. More importantly, why does anyone care what a woman is doing to her hair as long as she feels comfortable with it? Now, with a weave, people are shocked when I say things that don't conform to their stereotype of the European-identified, self-hating, confused Black sister.

Sometimes, though, I'm the one who's shocked. Recently, a man I'd just met looked at my straight-textured weave that hangs past my shoulder blades, and said, "April, whatever you do, don't cut your hair unless you ask me first. I just *love* your hair!" When I told my mother about his boldness, she retorted, "Since he likes it so much, why didn't you just tell him that you could send him a couple of packs in the mail?"

But with this hair also comes a lot of negative connotations. While Beyoncé, Tyra, and Naomi are considered beautiful with their weaves, regular Black women are often bashed and called out for "lying." I feel like some people, particularly Black people, consider me fake because my hair is fake. Or that I am this high-maintenance, glamour Barbie doll. An old friend from graduate school, who knew me with the braids, actually outright questioned my character because I hadn't let my hair go "free and natural." I just looked at him and shook my head, but said nothing. Because I had never thoughtlessly interrogated him about the connection between his mind and his 'do, I didn't see why he deserved my explanation. If I hadn't been insulted, I would have told him that the braids and ponytail attachment had broken off my hair and that I wanted to give it a chance to grow and repair. I may have even mentioned that I am lazy and love the ease and versatility. Instead, I simply reminded myself of the fun I was having, the hang-ups that I had moved past, and how my identity was far too complex to neatly guess at because of the way I styled what rested on top of my head.

April Yvonne Garrett is the president and CEO of April & Associates, an image-consulting firm. She is also the founder and director of the Groundwork Institute for Civic Dialogue.

APPLES AND PEARS

Tomika Anderson

Photo by G. Giraldo.

From the moment four years ago when I stepped off the plane in Montego Bay, I felt like a bona fide celebrity. Forgetting about my windblown hair, shiny face, and wrinkled clothes, I got lost in the lusty eyes of the sun-kissed Romeos roaming the airport—my thick figure and ample breasts met with raised brows, knowing winks, and smiles. I was about to autograph a few passports, or at least take a bow, when this gorgeous, dreadlocked passerby gave me a Colgate smile and officially welcomed me to the island. I could only stand there, cheesing like an idiot, trying desperately to recall the last time I'd felt so damned good.

To this day, Jamaica—a nation infamous for its worship of the portly female form—remains my Promised Land. Carrying more than 225 pounds on my 5'5", size 18, apple-shaped frame, back in New York City—home of the literally starving artist and pretzel-thin actress wannabe—I don't elicit anywhere near the kind of size-affirming attention that I love to get from men, lusty or not.

On hot summer days, my oversized T-shirt and sweatpants—lost in a sea of tanks-tops, bare midriffs, and booty-cutters—make me practically invisible to men out on the Manhattan street. Other times, I'm treated so rudely that I wish I were invisible. I get lewd comments from strangers about the violent bounce of my H-cup breasts as I scurry past. Or I'm told point-blank to "move my fat ass," something this crabby White man told me to do three years ago as I ambled amid a crush of fast-moving tourists in Times Square. When I make a rare appearance at my favorite hip-hop club with my three main homegirls—the largest of whom is a size 10—I'm the one who gets stuck grinding the broke, sweat suit–clad, strobe-light honey while my peeps back it up to the six-figure Brooks Brothers–clad cuties. While I don't hate on my girls, I sometimes think, *Damn, will one of these diamond-studded Negroes ever swing my way?* This type of man—whose multiple degrees and heavy pockets translate into easy access to the woman of his choice—seems to only be searching for the perfect size 5 to show off at the company picnic. For him, I often assume, even the fly, curvy, Jill Scott/Angie Stone types won't fit the bill. So to increase my odds of finding Mr. Right, I've posted headshot-only profiles on dating websites. Over the years, sites catering to the "large and luscious" have been my big salvation.

I've always been a big girl. Broad-shouldered with large arms and full "mother's breasts" since the eighth grade, the running joke among my average-sized parents and siblings was that minus the shoulder pads, I resembled an

NFL linebacker. As if it weren't enough to be the body double of William "The Refrigerator" Perry, I also had the misfortune of being the only Black girl in middle school who'd been skipped by the ass fairy. My pretty face, dimpled smile, and a head full of thick, curly hair didn't excuse the fact that I suffered from flat-butt syndrome. Because of my butt, inherited from my mom's side of the family, along with my big boobs, I was teased mercilessly. One of my pimply classmates even called me "slopey," because he said my ass sloped inward. So while many of the other sistas were filling out into that sexy pear shape Black women are known for, I was just a lonely apple, bulky up top with stick-legs at the bottom.

It was around middle school when I discovered how a half a box of Twinkies could ease the pain. Forsaking my mom's nutritious bag lunches for daytime feasts of cafeteria chicken nuggets, fries, and a honey bun, over time the pounds started to pile on. And no matter how physically active I became—in high school I ran track and played the four-spot on the varsity basketball team—my athleticism couldn't outdo my diet. I loved to eat junk food, and still do.

Self-conscious from years of schoolyard jokes and my parent's well-intentioned but often unnecessarily severe tirades over my weight, today I find myself sneakily consuming the foods I know are loaded with calories. If I'm at McDonald's with my friends, I'll be sure to whisper my request for the checkout girl to supersize my Extra Value Meal. When my best friend, to whom I constantly complain about my weight, is not looking, I'll smother my pork chops in gravy. And I'm far more likely to load my baked potato with margarine and sour cream than to eat it plain. My habits wouldn't be that bad if I didn't indulge all the time, but the truth is that I do. I sacrifice health for flavor, and to top it all off, I often overeat, which makes it ten times worse.

Despite my consistent weight sabotage, there are times when the reality of what I'm doing to my body kicks in, and hard. Not too surprisingly, I usually experience most of my moments of remorse when I'm out clothes shopping. Department store fitting rooms are like torture chambers to me. Standing naked in front of the mirror, I kick myself for all the days I chose the pizza over the chicken Caesar salad. I hate my humongous, droopy breasts; the tubing around my midsection; and the loose, flabby skin that's gathered in bunches on my lower back. I detest my butt, which, although wide, cuts a pancake silhouette. I abhor my round face and teacher-fat arms. I despise my thighs, which rub together hard enough to ignite a forest fire. I hate the fact that I can't jog up to my fourth-floor walk-up apartment without wheezing. I'm pissed that I have to choose between expensive-ass fashions for chicks my size from Lane Bryant, The Avenue, and Ashley Stewart or cheap floral muumuus from Macy's. Some days I even hate on my chubby Black and boriquen sistren from Washington Heights, Harlem, and The Bronx—damn them for being able to rock those Spandex booty-cutters and cleavage-spillers without shame.

Worst of all, I hate that I loathe my otherwise healthy body that God has given me. I'm ashamed because I feel I've dishonored myself (and Him) by allowing myself to be fat. Not once have I managed to stick to a diet—Weight Watchers, Atkins, the Zone, or any other weight-loss program—or lasted more than a month on any new workout regime. Although I know I'm practically welcoming the early onset of diabetes, heart disease, cancer, and stroke—physical ailments that befall far too many Black women—I feel powerless to stop. Sometimes I just don't believe I'll ever be able to get out of my fat-filled rut. I've lived like this for years, and I simply don't know any other way. I know it's not as simple as watching calories, cutting back on carbs, and working out—I've tried to do that time and again—it's about having the patience and courage to turn it all around.

A year ago, I decided to enlist some help from a psychotherapist in my fight to save the skinny girl inside me. She's helped me to understand that I can't transform my body until I transform my mind. Because I'm an emotional eater, she says my task is to let go of the rage I've felt toward my parents all these years, for always lecturing me about my weight (which they still do). I have to admit to myself how much of an impact the ridicule I endured in high school had on my self-esteem. And I have to refuse to believe the lies I've told myself for so long, that I really feel fine the way I am and that change is impossible. That if I'm not beautiful in the eyes of a man, then I'm not beautiful at all. Or worst of all (in my mind), that no brotha will ever be able to see past my chubby exterior and love me for what's on the inside.

Well, no brothas except maybe for the ones in my neighborhood of Crown Heights, Brooklyn. There's truly no place like home—second only to Flatbush as the biggest Caribbean neighborhood in the city, fortunately for West Indian and African American women like myself, there's no shortage of men who'd like nothing more than to bask in the glory of a pretty, plus-sized mama. I feel the love emanate from them every day on the block—when I walk up the street to buy groceries at the nearest bodega or go around the corner for Chinese takeout. Approached frequently by men of varying ages, sizes, and nationalities—tall, slender Indian Trinis; short, robust Jamaicans; muscular Bajans; and stout Grenadian men whose looks range from preppy, thuggish, unattractive, or downright fine—in B.K. I've got the virtual pick of the litter. But as soon as I jump on the Manhattan-bound 3 train, literally expanding the scope of my world, I feel my sexual power begin to slip away. In no time, I am once again reduced to being a fat chick who's held captive by her fears of rejection. In time, I'm hoping to change that.

Last summer I met a tall, slim, and handsome grad school student on a popular dating website. After three months of dating, with plenty of intense kissing and petting along the way, he became my boyfriend. And then came the moment I had dreaded the most—the night of our first sexual encounter. Tearing off my T-shirt and jeans so I could dive underneath the blankets, I damn near had a panic attack as I thought about what was to come. I really, really liked this guy, and I couldn't bear the thought that after he got one good look at my flat ass and Jell-O-pudding-pop tummy, he'd no longer want me. Paranoid, I watched him undress. He was so beautiful, with his smooth, fudge skin; ivory-colored teeth; and taut, athletic frame. I thought, *What on earth is he going to think of my body?* I couldn't help but to reminisce on all my sexual experiences gone wrong. I thought back to the skinny Latin lover three years before who later told his boy that the only reason he'd slept with me was to find out "what it was like to have sex with a big girl." Or my one-time encounter with the Puerto Rican papi who, prodding my juicy belly, asked, "What is that?"

With all my insecurities laid bare in front of my new lover, I felt incredibly self-conscious. While he was gentle—he took his time, playing with my hair, caressing my face, and kissing my neck—I just couldn't relax, thinking about everything he was seeing. I froze when his hand brushed my stomach, and I quickly pulled away from him every time he ran a finger up my cottage-cheese thigh. Eventually giving up on enjoying myself, as I had so many times before, I decided to fake my pleasure and just focus on pleasing him. When it was over, I turned my back to him, pretending to be too tired to talk.

It was months before I would build up the nerve to share my feelings of inadequacy with my boyfriend. Intentionally dropping my guard, I explained to him how my crappy body image had always interfered with my ability to relax and enjoy sex. I told him about the flat-ass jokes, about how I hated having my tummy touched, and about some of the mean things men had said to me over the years. We even laughed about how I always made sure I had easy access to my nightgown during sex, just in case I had to get out of bed and walk past him to get to the bathroom.

What he said to me then changed my life.

"You're crazy," he said, incredulous. "You're beautiful. Yeah, you've got a little meat here and there, but I love it. I love the way you look in your clothes. I love how your body feels, and the way you fit in my arms. You're comfortable, just like my little teddy bear, and I love you," he said for the first time.

As if he'd broken some kind of invisible spell, I started sobbing. No one had ever told me that my body was beautiful. Ever. I'd always felt that my body was unattractive and convinced myself that because of this, I wasn't entirely lovable. In that moment I got to see myself through the loving eyes of someone who wasn't judging me on being this hot piece of ass, but on who I was as this entire package. A whole person, and a beautiful one at that. Reflecting on that moment a year later, I realize how much the gift he gave continues to inspire me.

It also spurred me to action. A few months ago I joined Overeaters' Anonymous, a twelve-step program designed to help people alter their unhealthy relationships with food. This support group meets once a week. I signed up for swimming and aerobics at my neighborhood YWCA, rejoicing in the fellowship I found with other women who were also struggling to transform their bodies, and, in the process, their spirits. Finally trashing the broken record playing in my head—the one that tells me I'll be fat for life—I'm singing a new song now, and it's one that's filled with hope and redemption. If it takes the rest of my life, I'm going to work on feeling good about myself and accepting my body, no matter what size I am.

Besides, too many more trips to Jamaica would put a serious strain on my budget.

Tomika Anderson is a freelance writer living in Brooklyn, New York. Her work has appeared in such magazines as *Essence, Vibe, Time Out New York,* and *Entertainment Weekly.*

FEMME INVISIBILITY

Laini Madhubuti

Photo by G. Giraldo.

I am attracted to a woman who wears her sexuality on her sleeve. One you can tell is "kinda funny" by the way she swaggers rather than walks and puts her breasts away because they don't define her.

I'm constantly entranced by this woman who exudes her own form of gender rebellion because she has the audacity to be herself, to saunter down the street knowing that an assault of verbal and visual messages will tell her that she's not beautiful.

I love a woman who hears, "You'd be such a pretty girl if you'd just put on a little makeup and wear a skirt every once in a while." She hears this plea of sorts from straight folks and even the queer women who are supposed to be her allies. They can see her beauty without the traditionally feminine trappings but need to make themselves feel at ease with the way she's challenged their sense of normalcy.

I am comfortable with her unplanned protest.

While I'm drawn to someone who has no particular allegiance to the female pronoun, I look like your typical straight girl—like all my straight friends. I wear the same revealing tops and curve-embracing bottoms, love the same huge, eye-catching earrings, suffer in the same senseless stilettos, have the same *pop pop* strut that drives the boys crazy. My version of beauty makes everyone feel comfortable. I fit right into the Black heterosexual beauty ideal.

I sweep my sleepy eyes with mascara each day and brighten up my full lips with a blindingly shiny lip-gloss. I spend three to four hours a month twisting my locks into perfectly coiled ropes that rest on my slender shoulders. The hips that my partner de-emphasizes are the ones that I flaunt. After much confusion, I've learned that these hips are nothing to work or starve off, but what, along with my long legs, make me my grandmother's twin.

Even if I didn't indulge my lifelong love of makeup and clothes, I'd still be considered extra-feminine. All my life, I have been branded delicate, graceful, and dainty because I'm a tall girl with long limbs who walks with her spine straight and her head in the air.

Living as a straight woman, I didn't think twice about my innate femininity. I acted like a "lady," and I knew how people on the south side of Chicago, where I was born; in Atlanta, where I went to college; and in New York City, where I work, would perceive me.

But entering the queer community, where femininity isn't the rule and labels abound, I didn't know where I fit. My new queer identity didn't change the way I felt about my physical body; I was still confident in its beauty. But I began to question how I showcased it, wondered what registered when an attractive woman glanced at it.

I became very envious of women who identified strongly with their masculinity because they, unlike me, were not assumed to be straight (even if they were). Among "femme aggressives," "butches," "soft butches," "bois," and "transfolk," I saw my girly sensibility as the opposite of queer identity. I knew I loved women; I just thought I didn't *look* like I loved them.

During that blind journey from trepid bi to loud queer, I'd frequent clubs alone and hide in corners just observing my new family. After about two months of feeling like an outsider, I ditched my favorite red lipstick and started wearing white ribbed tank tops that showcased my torso but muted my femininity. Thankfully, during this phase, I learned to like myself unmasked. As I immersed myself in this new community, I began to attract people—including an annoyingly aggressive butch girlfriend who decided where I fit on the queer women's identity continuum: I was a "femme."

Coming out of my ex's mouth, "femme" sounded like a put-down. We femmes were supposed to be lite; obsessed with clothes, hair, and makeup; and treated like our primary purpose was to compliment butches.

I, an unapologetic feminist, hadn't left the sexism built into hetero roles just to get locked into some gay version of the same thing. Still, I'm ashamed to say there were times I didn't stand as strong as I should have. In response to being treated like a weakling, I tried to "butch up." Sometimes I'd sit with my legs a little wider. I'd find myself boppin' instead of gliding. I altered the way I carried my body to convince the world—and myself—that I wasn't "just a femme."

And when I walked in the heterosexual world, I secretly cursed my femme invisibility. It's funny how the morning's sexy would become the nighttime's naked. When it was warm and the catcallers got bolder, I felt exposed and nearly hysterical. I wanted to appear off-limits and tough, like the women I found so attractive. At the same time, I knew my femme invisibility shielded me from a different, violent kind of harassment. I'd remember fifteen-year-old Sakia Gunn, the Newark, New Jersey, teenager who was stabbed to death for telling a twenty-nine-year-old man that she was a lesbian and not interested. My innate femininity kept the power dynamics between me and these men intact. My femme invisibility didn't disrupt their sense of normalcy, so they didn't need to attack me to make their world all right again.

It has taken more than three years, several relationships, and loads of new friends who identify all over the map for me to learn that my girly, switchin', delicate, curvy self is queer enough on her own. I'm queer because of whom I love, not because of the way I look. This is particularly important when I meet someone new. People, no matter their sexual preference, tend to take in the way I adorn and carry my body and spit out incorrect assumptions about whom I kiss.

Because I have to, for my sanity, I remind myself daily that labels say more about the person doing the assigning than they do about the assignee.

Folks need to find a box to put you in, and they need for you to stay there, safely within their realm of comprehension. Now, I don't stay.

Laini Madhubuti has contributed to *The Source*, BET.com, and *Ana Castro*, a magazine for queer women of color. She currently works in publicity at The Schomburg Center for Research in Black Culture and moderates the listserve Femme Menace.

FEELING PRETTY

Jill Scott
as told to Karen R. Good,
Ayana Byrd, and
Akiba Solomon

Photo by Keith Major.

Each of us is like a blade of grass, with all of the fantastic nuances that the Lord has given us. So to want to look like someone else is frightening. I think that's just people deciding that there's no beauty inside, that their beauty has to come from the outside.

Looking at the outside, at the media, we're continually being shown the same kind of woman. It's as if God just created one kind of flower. But how do you compare a red rose to a white rose? Or a white rose to a daisy?

Lighter skinned women are prized to a degree. You have to have a certain kind of body and the soft hair—you gotta have the hair. If you have light eyes, oh my God! But if you're a brown-skinned girl, then good luck. It seems like you have to straighten your hair and expose your body to measure up. When I say these things, people ask, "Why you hatin' on light-skinned people?"

I'm not hatin' on any damn body. I don't have time for that. I'm light-skinned and I used to be a size 6, so I know.

The truth is, there is a history of slavery that just doesn't seem to go away—a history of the lighter women working in the house while the darker women had their babies in the field. As much as most of us want to say that we've moved on, a lot of that stuff is still sitting in our stomachs. We still experience that hatred, still say that the lighter person is better than the darker one. It makes me think about my grandmother; she's so dark, they renamed her blue. Her skin color is gorgeous, yet when I tell her she's beautiful she says, "Oh, you just love me."

No matter what you look like, the media can make you feel like you're not pretty enough. So when I talk about positivity, I'm not only telling others, I'm also telling myself. I'm just a person, slowly and surely walking away from old hurts and pains, trying to learn something every day.

I feel most beautiful when I'm not really sweatin' it, those times when I'll walk past a mirror and think, "There's a pretty girl right there." Because this is who I am. My fingers work, my toes work, my ears are pretty good, and I can see in both directions. My freedom comes with knowing that this body has been blessed.

Jill Scott is a platinum-selling recording artist, Grammy-winning songwriter, published poet, and actress. Her latest album is *Beautifully Human*.

PLAYING
THE
VIXEN

Margeaux Watson

Photo by G. Giraldo.

June 24, 1991

Dear Diary,

Last night I was at my friend Brandon's house, hanging out in his room, as usual. At first, we were just laying on the bed, watching TV. But then we started to make out. Soon he was completely naked. I let him feel my breasts and suck on them. I don't know why, but I just let him. It got more intense and then he asked me if I wanted to do it.

At first, I said no but then changed my mind. He put on a condom then he pulled off my shorts and panties and then he [lay] on top of me and he put it in. It hurt so bad, and he asked me if I wanted to stop. I told him no, so we continued but it still hurt, and he asked me if I wanted to cover up my mouth with something so that I would be quiet. He told me that I should kiss his neck but I couldn't because it hurt too bad. Soon, I began to cry. I don't think that he noticed though. He went in really hard, harder than before, so hard that I let out a yell. Then he pulled out and that was it. We didn't say anything.

I felt so bad. I felt like a slut. I couldn't believe that I had just had sex with somebody that I'd known for less than a month.

I had to be home soon so I put on my clothes and he put on some shorts and walked me to the front door. I gave him a hug good-bye, and I felt him watching me as I walked down his block. I'm glad he didn't walk me home because it gave me time to think about a lot of things. I thought about what kind of person I am. I thought about what people would think if they knew. And I thought about why I did it. Why? I guess because last year when I was fourteen, I was fat and my hair was never really nice looking, and the guys I messed with were ugly and I did just about anything they wanted because I thought they wouldn't like me if I didn't.

Then I changed. I starved myself for a while and I lost a lot of weight. I started wearing makeup and doing my hair. I changed the way I dressed, and I was a brand-new person by my freshman year. Then I made a promise to myself that I would not mess with any ugly people this year. At first, I was discouraged because I didn't mess with anybody for eight months. But then I met Shomari. Then after Shomari, my dream came true and I met Charles, Leetray, Anthony, Brandon, and Jerome. Five guys liked me, and none of them were ugly. I couldn't believe it. That was more than I expected.

Growing up, the only thing worse than feeling like a misfit was looking like one. I'd always been a big girl. Not fat or muscular. Just thick. Juicy, if you will. I get my voluptuous shape from my mother, a proud woman who was built this way even before she had my sisters and me. In junior high, I skipped the training-bra stage. By the end of the eighth grade, I'd ballooned from a 34B to a 38C.

The following school year I felt so out of place socially that I began projecting those anxieties onto my bigger-than-average breasts, curvy hips, and thick thighs. It was horrible. All I wanted to do was feel and look the same as everyone else, but I stood out more. My classmates' acceptance and approval meant everything to me because I didn't have a social life beyond school. (The kids in my neighborhood, who all attended the same predominantly Black public and Catholic schools, taunted me for being "a White girl" as frequently as my Black classmates did.)

Like most teenagers, I internalized my distress and anxiety because I assumed neither my parents nor my sisters could understand or help me. I was embarrassed to be struggling with my weight; I felt it was an awful, ugly secret. And so I attempted to deal with it on my own by developing a rigid workout schedule: in addition to aerobics classes, intramural soccer, and swimming, five days a week I did forty minutes on the StairMaster followed by forty minutes of Nautilus and weight training. Within a matter of months, I dropped from a size 15/16 to an 11/12.

Everyone—including my friends and family—applauded my new svelte waistline and the muscle tone I had achieved in my arms, legs, and back. It felt great to shorten my school uniform to the length of a miniskirt so that my boxer shorts could hang below it like the rest of my classmates. Still, exercising did nothing to minimize my curves; it accentuated them more than ever. That's when I noticed that older guys seemed more attracted to my body than boys my own age. At school, there was a groundskeeper who would stop what he was doing whenever I walked by and leer at me. Because he was handsome and in his twenties, my friends thought it was so cool when he would say things to me like, "Girl, your body is everything a man my age wants in a woman." But his advances only made me feel like prey.

Looking back, I'm sure most boys my age, insecure about their own pubescent woes, were too intimidated by my rapidly developed physique to approach me. But at the time, I felt hopelessly fat and ugly around them.

At thirteen, as my hormones kicked into high gear and ignited my sex drive, I became a fixture on the local teen club scene. These clubs were the perfect hangout for predatory college students and guys in their early- to mid-twenties with an appetite for immature girls who looked grown. Young, horny, and easily impressed, I was charmed by their vulgar advances.

Around this time I began portraying myself as a flirtatious vixen—because that's how people perceived me, I figured I better act the part. For me, that meant not being labeled a "dick tease"—you know, the type of girl who always flaunted yet never actually delivered the goods. No, I wanted to be esteemed by my suitors for being young, hot, and uninhibited. Which is why at fifteen, I was among the first wave of my friends to have sex. I lost my virginity to a nineteen-year-old I met at a club, and I continued to date older guys throughout high school. (In the senior class poll of my yearbook, I was voted "Best with Men" over "Best with Boys.") I thought I was hot shit because I was dating guys who were old enough to drive fancy cars and have their own apartments, though in reality most of them lived with their parents. Meanwhile, my own parents were in the dark because I never brought my boyfriends home to meet them, and I always lied about their ages.

Even though I tried to act as grown as my body looked, I wound up facing a bunch of adult problems that I wasn't prepared to handle. The first installment in a brutal series of formative incidents occurred when I was seventeen. I was secretly dating a twenty-four-year-old DJ who spun at all the hottest parties. One day after school, we were sitting on his waterbed talking shit and drinking hideously cheap liquor when he suddenly pounced on me. I wasn't afraid to sleep with him because we had been having sex for a couple of months; I was just surprised by the way he attacked me.

Without warning or warming up, he ripped off my panties and began ramming away inside of me. I screamed, tried to fight him off, and pleaded with him to stop, but my distress only excited him more. At one point, he looked directly into my eyes and asked, "Am I hurting you?" I whimpered, "Yes." He groaned with demented delight and replied, "Good. I want to hurt you!"

The episode lasted only a few ugly minutes, but it seemed like an eternity. After it was over, I lay there in silence, stunned by what had just happened. He abruptly grabbed my hand and yanked me off the bed. He wouldn't let me leave through the front door; instead, he steered me to the alley. Before I walked home, he gripped my arm and warned, "Don't even think about telling anybody what just happened. No one would believe you, anyway. They would just think you're some young girl who has a crush on me." I believed him, never said a word, and dismissed the incident as an unfortunate side effect of fooling around with older men. Rather than crying foul, I convinced myself that I needed to toughen up by learning to disassociate my emotions from sex to live up to the coquettish image of myself that I had concocted. Even worse, I continued to "date" the bastard off and on for about a year.

NAKED

Spring 1994

When did my descent begin? I'm unsure. I think it was when my body began transforming. When breasts no longer needed training and hips curved down into thickening thighs and I was the reflection in the eyes of boys and men passing me by, looking me over, sizing me up. Or was it when I committed the ultimate sin and allowed a doctor go in and vacuum the unborn, innocent life I conceived. Because I was too young. Because he abandoned us. Because of the fear that dwelled within me.

I saw disappointment in my parents' eyes and heard it in their whys. They made my decision for me because my irresponsibility coupled with immaturity completely invalidated my voice and left me with no choice but theirs.

On that table, hysterical fears provoked tears and choked my screams as I tried to listen to the nurse's instructions: "Calm down. Relax. It will all be over in less than five minutes."

But she lied, because it isn't over. The girl who lay down on that table and spread her knees apart died at the moment the humming metal machine was switched off and she could feel no more tugging and scraping inside her womb. All that remained of her were the tears she had shed uncontrollably just before she slipped away, praying they would wash her away to some distant shore where salvation was waiting. That girl died, giving birth to me—a frightened young and naïve woman.

In the wake of my abortion, I stopped wearing makeup, cut off all my chemically straightened hair, and began to grow dreadlocks. I also gave away all my clothes, replacing my trendy suburban wardrobe with baggy bohemian thrift and grunge attire. I thought that by transforming my appearance, I could somehow wipe away all the inner ugliness. I felt dirty and fast because I was only seventeen and had already slept with at least five guys and been pregnant. I didn't want to be sexy anymore; I just wanted to contain my body, which I continued to blame for these experiences. By adopting a more boyish look, I hoped to establish a new, less sexual energy in my interactions with men. I also developed a penchant for controlling and emotionally abusive men. Looking back, I can see that I was punishing myself for having the abortion; I believed I could heal myself by allowing them to mistreat me.

I carried these feelings of shame from Baltimore to New York City, where I started Columbia University the following fall. Three months into my freshman year, my past repeated itself: an upperclassman who I thought was my friend raped me. He was a star athlete and the most popular guy on campus. I was going through an "ugly phase"—my dreadlocks were short and fuzzy and my wardrobe consisted of Timberland boots, Carhartt construction jeans, and baggy sweatshirts—so the night he called and invited me to hang out in his dorm room, I eagerly accepted, assuming that because of my less-than-fetching appearance, he genuinely wanted to be "just friends."

I thought he was joking when he told me to remove my clothes minutes after I had arrived. He wasn't. The room was so small that I couldn't run past him and out the door. The music from his stereo was blaring so that no one would have heard me if I screamed. Intimidated by his muscular 6'3", 250-pound frame, I shed my clothes and sat on the edge of his bed. He grabbed the back of my head with one massive hand and shoved my face down. He commanded me to "suck his dick" and wrapped one of his enormous thighs around my neck so that I didn't have a choice. After a while, he instructed me to lie on the floor. He put on a condom, climbed on top of me, and grinded away inside my dry vagina.

This rape convinced me that no matter how I dressed it up or down, there was something overtly and potently sexual about my body that men couldn't resist and I couldn't control. I sank into a dark period of depression.

Winter 1995

I don't want to be alone. I'm scared of what I think when there's no sound. I'm afraid of what I learn when I'm not studying.

Over the past ten years, as I've crawled from beneath the rubble of despair that had been piling up since I was a teen, I have mastered the ability to emotionally disconnect from sex. Through a process of trial and error, I have conceived a set of dating and mating rules to live by: no gratuitous foreplay, no kissing during sex, always maintain the home-court advantage in bed, and absolutely no sleepovers. If I'm friends with a guy I truly care about, I won't have sex with him. If I'm in a sexual relationship with a guy, I won't be friends with him beyond the bedroom. In short, I have shifted the power dynamic in my favor by any means necessary.

I now recognize and am addressing my paralyzing fear of intimacy. But since graduating college in 1998, I have spent most of my energy achieving professional and financial success as an entertainment journalist. Today, I am well known by my peers and regarded by urban socialites as a party-hopping tastemaker.

As petty and juvenile as it may sound, I feel like I belong for the first time in my life. Professional success and social acceptance have eliminated the anxieties that I projected onto my body as a teenager.

At 29 and 5'7", I now wear a 38DD bra and can fit into most anything in the size 10 to 14 range. I don't work out much but through watching what I eat and frequently dieting, I've been able to maintain a classic hourglass figure: big perky titties, stomach flat enough to display midriff, tiny high waist, large ass, and thunder thighs. I love what I see when I stand naked in front of my mirror each morning, and I'm proud to flaunt it by wearing clothes that accentuate my best assets, namely my boobs and my booty.

Sure, the animalistic, objectifying way most guys respond to my body sometimes makes me feel like sexy parts rather than a beautiful whole. But unlike my vulnerable teenage self—a growing thing ripened too soon who felt sexually and emotionally victimized by puberty—I now recognize and appreciate my body for what it is: a living, breathing, gorgeous instrument of power. And although there's not much I can do to stop the unwanted chorus of catcalls that erupts whenever I step outside my front door, I am no longer intimidated by it, either. Besides, they're right: I am one sexy MF—thunder thighs and all!

Margeaux Watson is a correspondent at *Entertainment Weekly* and has written for a range of publications, including *Rolling Stone*; *Vibe*; *O, The Oprah Magazine*; and *GQ*.

COLD TURKEY

asha bandele

Sometimes I look at Nisa, this four-year-old child of mine, and am stunned by her absolute love of her body. Rare is the day that goes by that she doesn't ask me to pick her up so she can look at the whole of herself in the mirror, and exclaim: "Look at me, Mommy! Look at me!" And I do, knowing I must have been like that once, a person completely happy with myself, happy with what I look like.

Finally, my body is no longer the battleground it was for two decades. I couldn't even tell you what I weigh because I am clear how tyrannical that digital numbers on the scale are, how they dictated the course and mood of my life. But even as I celebrate the place I'm in now, I never allow myself to forget how I arrived here.

Even a cursory glance through the newspaper tells me that there are countless things far worse to be than an overweight eighteen-year-old. But when I was an overweight teenaged girl living in the size 2, Calvin Klein–jeans world of urban America, no one could convince me of that. Even today, in my thirties, when I think about being eighteen and fat, it still takes my breath away, the hurt and loneliness and shame I felt then. It haunted me, kept me too often from saying what I had to say, terrified I'd hear, "Who cares what your fat ass thinks?" In the face of that pain, macaroni and cheese, Oreos, fried chicken, and ice cream seemed less like the problem than they did a salve. They never judged me.

I was in my early twenties when I couldn't take it anymore, the extra fifty pounds and the indignity I associated with it. I'd begun living bicoastal, shuttling regularly between California and New York. In New York, especially in the Black neighborhood where I lived, my size-18 body didn't make me stand out. I only had to deal with weight issues when I ventured into the sleek Manhattan world where my office was located. San Francisco had no hiding place for me; everyone was going to the gym, eating vegetarian food, jogging at 6 each morning. I wanted to join their ranks, become a picture of health and fitness, wear tank tops all the time.

At the suggestion of a friend, I joined a gym and consulted with a staff member. Although he was certified as a personal trainer, his advice was several cuts below terrible. I still remember him looking at my body clinically and asking me how many calories I ate a day. I had no idea. I had no concept of what I ate each day and had certainly never thought to count a calorie. I didn't even have the cultural context to think that way. In my family, you might get called fat, but at the end of the day, food was still a reward. In fact, it was an insult not to eat, or to eat delicately. But on that day with the trainer, whom I now believe was a complete madman, I was told that a woman my size didn't need to eat more than 500 or 600 calories a day. I agreed, bought a calorie counter at my local drugstore, and that's when it started—my obsession with starvation. I never was able to get my daily intake down to 500 calories, but for at least two years—I still have the food journals to prove it—I ate 800 to 1,000 calories. Eight hundred was a good day; 1,000 meant I was a pig. I monitored every fat gram, every protein gram, every gram of fiber and carbohydrate. The weight came off in a matter of months. But not just the fifty pounds I set out to lose. First I dropped an additional ten, and then ten became twenty, which became thirty-five. In about six months I went from a size 18 to a size 4.

Never mind that for my 5'6" height and large frame, a size 10 was appropriate. I thought I looked great, plus I loved my self-control. Starvation made me feel strong. I felt that power even on the day I ran into a girlfriend who hadn't seen me in months. She stared at me, and in a horrified whisper asked, "asha, are you sick? Do you have cancer?" I laughed, said no—and actually felt complimented. I babbled on about working out, eating "right," and being on a path to total health and fitness. She told me right then and there, as my little sister and lover later confirmed, that my twenty-something face had begun to develop wrinkles because the emaciation was so profound. Eventually my sister asked me to go to a doctor, to get on a better plan. But I was a freelance writer finishing a master's degree. I had no insurance, and truth be told, no inclination. I didn't see myself then as they did. Only later, when I looked at photographs of myself from that period, can I see where I was headed. But in that moment when I was asked if I had cancer, I just reassured my friend. As a matter of fact, I told her, I was about to quit smoking, which I did cold turkey, one overcast November morning about eight years ago.

For months afterward I felt absolutely incredible. Not physically—physically, I was tired—but emotionally. I saw myself as woman with no vices, a rarity in a society so defined by its addictions. I felt like I was better than others, nearly a miracle woman. I didn't smoke, didn't drink, didn't make midnight forays into the fridge, worked out five or six times a week, and was training myself to run the New York marathon.

Here's one of those particularly-irritating-because-it's-so-damn-true clichés: all you can expect in life is the unexpected. In the midst of feeling good, albeit hungry, my thyroid gland went crazy—there's no medical explanation why this happens, it just does. My shoulder-length hair fell out; I was often short of breath; my emotions rocked me. I borrowed some money and went to see a doctor who told me my gland was working against me and would have to be removed, which is what happened about a week after the diagnosis. Now I take, as I will have to for the rest of my life, a daily chemical replacement. The drugs have achieved a semblance of balance with my body, but in those initial months following the procedure, my metabolism just stopped; I gained thirty-five pounds in a single summer. How could that happen after all my work, all those hungry days, all those damn steamed vegetables? But most of all, what was I going to do? Doctors and nutritionists—none of whom knew my relationship with food, only my current desperation—told me to just eat right and exercise, which made me crazy because I believed I was doing that. "Cut back a little then," one doctor suggested before shooing me out of his office. But I couldn't figure out how to eat any less than I already did. There was no more time in the day for me to work out. How could I get my already stringent caloric intake, about 1,000 on most days, 1,200 on holidays, closer to zero?

The answer came by way of a television drama that I happened upon. I'm sure it was meant to be viewed as a cautionary tale, but I saw it as an escape route. I sat and watched a teenaged character throw up nearly everything she ate. Yes, it was disgusting. But the doctors didn't take my fears seriously. The people closest to me, in particular my lover, thought I looked better with the extra pounds. No one understood except this fictional character in a TV drama. So at twenty-eight—ten years past what therapists consider the danger zone—I became a bulimic. After nearly every meal, I would excuse myself, go to the bathroom, kneel in front of my toilet, put two fingers or sometimes three down my throat, and throw up everything I ate. It was messy, and often difficult to manage those annoying times I was in a restaurant bathroom and some frustrated patron began knocking on the door asking if I was all right. But it was a pretty good solution, I thought. I even treated myself to some of my old favorite foods—in a manner of speaking.

Bulimia, like any other disorder, can't be hidden forever. My sister, a social worker, began noticing the marks on the backs of my hands—that's one of the things that happens when you're shoving three fingers down your throat several times a day. Your knuckles get cut on your teeth. She made me go to therapy, and I did, knowing each time I left the session I would be on my knees in the bathroom, expelling pizza, macaroni and cheese, french fries, whatever. My therapist knew this of course; I wasn't adept at fooling some-one trained to work with people who had eating disorders.

But for those first several weeks in counseling, she didn't confront me. We talked mostly about why I hated my body/myself, when the hate started, what had spun it out of control. I constantly tried to steer the conversation back to my missing thyroid, but she refused to allow our talks to occur at an arm's distance. During one exasperating session about six months into our work together, I whispered something about men I'd known when I was a child, what they did, where they touched, what they took, what they left be-hind. I told her, as briefly as I could, about the assault by my mother's col-league when I was seven. I told her how it positioned me sexually to enter the world, how it positioned me to hate this body of mine that had been used as a repository for perversion. I cried, but just as quickly as they came, the tears dried up. That was all so long ago, I said. I've already dealt with it. I'm over it now. She nodded and asked me what I thought the right amount of healing time should be for a wound you can't see and others don't acknowledge? I shrugged; it was getting uncomfortable. I was bored with my own drama. I went home, ate, and threw up.

Two weeks later, after a bout of real, not forced nausea, I discovered I was pregnant. When I told my therapist this—and that I wouldn't be coming back because I couldn't pay her and save for the baby all at the same time— she told me thought we should continue working together. When I insisted I couldn't, for the first time she really confronted me about my bingeing and purging, pointing to the marks still there on my knuckles. She suggested I read the chapter in her book about what bulimia can do to an unborn child.

I did; the bulimia ended right then, just like that. Really, it's the way I've always quit things, smoking, overeating—I go cold turkey, and try to keep moving forward. So there was no fanfare, no great struggle the day I knew I would never purge again. There was just the simple resolve that came with knowing that my body was here to do something really important, and that whatever else I'd done wrong, I was going to try as hard as I could to do the mommy thing right. I gave my heart, my energy, my body, to that child who was coming to me.

Once while I was lost in fit of insecurity, my daughter's father said if he could give me one gift, it would be for me to see myself in the way he saw me. "If only," he said, "you could look at yourself with my eyes." I never was able to achieve that with him. But pregnant, I was able to see my body through the spirit of my child. What she needed directed every choice I made. If I was hungry, I ate. If I needed to rest, I did. And if I needed to sit, legs open, shirt raised just above the waist, and rub or scratch my huge stomach, I did— pretty much anywhere I thought I wouldn't get arrested for it. Pregnant, I felt free. And there is nothing—no diet, no makeup, no designer gear—that will make a woman feel more beautiful than freedom. My body could no longer, and was no longer, expected to belong in a size 4 world. It belonged to itself, to the life growing inside me. It belonged to me. And that turned me on in a way I had never known. I'd never before felt so sexy, so fly, so damn woman as I did waddling around at nearly 200 pounds.

Nisa is four years old now, and the baby weight is gone. I watch what I eat, but I haven't kept a food journal since I found out I was pregnant. I don't work out much anymore, except to run behind my daughter. I couldn't tell you what I weigh or even what size I am since my clothes run the gamut between 6 and 12, depending on the designer. The body that carried my daughter has changed in so many ways since the day she was born, but the most significant thing remains. When I stand naked in a mirror now, I see my body as this incredible thing, stretch marks and all. I no longer measure myself according to standards I did not set up and do not control.

Now I see a body that grew a life, and that brought it forth, safe and healthy, into the world. Now the power and strength I feel comes not from starvation, skinniness, or running one more mile. I feel strong because this body of mine continues, despite extreme exhaustion, to engage life, to roll around in the floor with it, to cuddle up close and giggle, and to run with it and clean up after it. I feel strong because this body of mine is willing to embrace life—both mine and my child's—unrestrained and unashamed.

asha bandele is an award-winning author and poet. Her most recent book is *Daughter.* She lives in Brooklyn with her little girl, Nisa.

IN SEARCH OF . . .

(A Real-Life Body Play in Three Acts)

Rosemary Matthews

Photo courtesy of Rosemary Matthews.

Act I: 1950

There were no colored pinup girls. So at fourteen, I aspired to be a Betty. Pictured in her cardigan sweater buttoned down the back, blond Betty Grable and her protruding breasts were posted in GI lockers around the world. Betty set the standard for sexiness during World War II.

Now, I didn't need to be pinned up across the globe. I was fine with having my picture posted in the boys locker room at Newton High. But that was not to be. I was about 5'5", weighed 135 pounds and, by any stretch, was considered a big girl. I was not fat. I wasn't even husky. I was kind of country-girl strong. Because of my largeness and naivete, I was the butt of the boys' jokes. They called me Young Pony or, even meaner, Virgin Mary. Apparently, I was not sexy.

When all the other girls on my block started developing breasts, pubic hair, and pubescent prissiness, I was flat-chested and carefree. Their "aunts had come to visit," and I did not know what that meant or why they had to change because of it. I stayed the same old silly Rosemary, hanging upside down in the tree across the street, skirt covering my face, butt and stomach bare.

They thought I was disgusting doing this, so I stopped. I didn't think it was disgusting. I thought it was great. But I didn't want the others to put me down, so I gave up something that I truly loved for the sake of belonging.

Had I come up in a different time, I probably would have picketed for the rights of big girls to hang upside down from trees whenever they damned well felt like it. Instead, I retreated into a world of my own, feeling ill-equipped to cope when the more developed girls, including my younger sister, abandoned me during these terrible teasing times.

Once a day, four days a week, as we changed for gym, Newtown High School became a place of particular torture. I was the only girl still wearing an undershirt. I heard the snickers of the bra-wearers and after a while began cutting gym to avoid them. It was then that I took up smoking and pitching pennies behind the school.

Soon after I dropped out of gym class, I asked my aunt if she would buy me a training bra. I had heard that phrase somewhere and took it literally. It was a bra that would train my breasts to grow. She turned around and stared at me. It was a strange, blank, befuddled look, as if I had spoken in some unknown language. I remember hanging my head and walking away.

One bright day, the other girls and I were all outside just being fourteen-year-olds when a group of boys surrounded us. All of a sudden the attention turned to me. And my flat chest. Girls and boys alike took great delight in pointing out that I was the only girl who did not wear a bra. Mortified, I ran into the house and, for a few moments, just sat. Then a light went off in my head. *Aha! A bra!* If all I needed was a bra to shut them up, this was a problem that could be easily fixed.

I knew where bras were. Not just cute bras or training bras but *big* bras. So I dashed into my aunt's bedroom, dove into her top drawer, and pulled out what had to have been a 36D. I put it on and began adjusting straps. I still didn't look right, so I filled up the cups with stockings. Old, tattered stockings my aunt was going to use to stuff rag dolls.

To enhance the look, I applied some Broadway-thick makeup to my face. Then I found one of my aunt's cardigan sweaters and put it on backward, Betty-style. Accompanied by my tightest pair of Levis jeans, I was looking *good.* Sexy pinup-girl good. I was ready to face my tormentors and put them in their place.

Our house had a front door and a side door. For the best staging, I chose to emerge from the side door, sidle up to the front of the house, and shock the group: *Bam! Take that, you wimpy bra-wearing girls!* I almost made it to my mark, but one of the group turned around and saw me prematurely. By the time I reached the front of the house, they were all falling into the shrubs, just cracking up. The laughter was so loud that one of our adult neighbors came out to see what was going on.

The boys and girls simply pointed to me. The neighbor seemed stunned, frozen for what seemed like a whole minute. Then she led me back into the house and gently suggested that I take off my aunt's clothes and wash the garish makeup off my face. She must have said something to silence the audience gathered in front of the house because they dispersed.

Later on, my neighbor intercepted my aunt on her way home from work and told her what had happened. I think my aunt was torn between sympathy for me and her own embarrassment. I also suspect that she didn't know how to explain why my little sister had breasts and I didn't. My stunt made it clear that something needed to be done about me.

She took me to our family physician, a kind, elderly gentleman who treated everybody in Elmhurst, Queens. I think my aunt was actually concerned about my mental health but wasn't quite sure how to go about having me evaluated. After giving me a complete physical, the doctor pronounced me fit as a fiddle in spite of my flat chest. He gave me a little fatherly lecture about how lucky I was to be in good health. I didn't care. I just wanted to run away. To retreat into a world of my own where girls didn't let silly things like breasts and bras divide them. But then my aunt—the typically stern surrogate who took me in at three years old after my mother died—came to the rescue. She took me to a specialty shop on Jamaica Avenue to have a few padded bras custom-made for me. How healing it was to watch the saleswoman and my "mother" turn a mundane purchase into a chance to be creative, to correct one of nature's mistakes. I felt special as they measured me and fussed over the correct cup size. When they fastened the last hook of my new 32A padded bra, I felt as if the curse was lifted.

This act of kindness normalized my life. It allowed me to quit pitching pennies and smoking cigarettes behind the school and return to gym class.

Back on the block, where no one questioned my overnight curves, I finally became one of the girls. Now I was included in their conversations about boys and even had prospects of my own. Each time I would wear a cardigan sweater buttoned down Betty-style, I would feel as if I had arrived.

Act II: 1960

By age twenty-three, I was married, widowed by an accident, and the mother of two sons, ages two and three. I no longer aspired to be a pinup girl like Betty Grable. Now I was a Bed-Stuy beauty queen.

I did not work or go to school. I divided my time between mothering— my sons' socks always matched their outfits—and being a platinum blonde bombshell, courtesy of the finest beehive wig money could buy. During the day, I was a mother *par excellence*. When the sun set, it was on with the wig and some very sexy outfit and off to a glamorous Harlem party.

One summer afternoon changed all of that.

Strolling down Troy Avenue with my two impeccably dressed sons, I noticed this very tall, very dark, very nappy-headed Negro coming toward us. He tried to make eye contact with me, but I dismissed him. He was nothing; something to be avoided. As we neared one another on the narrow street, he didn't step aside as expected. He walked right into me, as if he were going to bump into me. Then he cracked up.

I looked around to see what was so funny. I *knew* he wasn't laughing at me. I looked behind me and to my left and right and didn't see anything happening. I looked down at my sons to see if one of them were doing something funny. The joke wasn't there either. By this moment, he was only inches away from my square of the sidewalk. He stopped short, gazed at my wig, and hissed, "Don't you know you are a *Black* woman?" Then he continued on his way.

I was stunned. I had no idea what he meant by "Black" because I was certainly yellow. This was 1960, back when Black was not a compliment. Not for the Negro and colored population and most certainly not for the redbones and high yellas like me. I was used to hearing, "Mmm, mmm, mmm! Yellow, yellow, you are *mellow*." I was all that, and everyone knew it. This black-skinned, need-to-go-home-and-comb-his-nappy-hair lunatic didn't matter. His amusement over my beehive was proof that he was a truly ignorant fool. Some days later I learned that this unkempt, ugly menace whom I had mistaken for one of the nuts running loose in Brooklyn was actually the new social worker at the Albany Houses, where I was living at the time.

I'm not sure how long it was after my meeting with Mr. Tall, Black, and Nappy that I saw Cicely Tyson on TV. She had all of her hair cut off. As I watched the show, chimes and gongs went off in my psyche.

At first I was a kind of like, *Ugh. What is up with that?* But as the show progressed, I began to think, *Umm, check out how different and beautiful she looks . . .* Then it clicked: *This* was how I would show Mr. Tall, Black, and Nappy that he couldn't mess with me! He thought he was so smart and deep, but I was going to show him. I was going to create an image. Vengeance would be mine!

The following morning, I went to the neighborhood barber and asked him to cut all of my hair off like Cicely Tyson's. He did not know who Cicely Tyson was and hadn't seen the TV show, so I just picked a style from one of the men's hair charts.

"Cut it like that," I said, pointing to a short natural.

"You mean all off, like a man's?" the barber asked incredulously.

"Right. All off, like a man's."

When I stepped out of that chair and onto the streets of Bedford Stuyvesant, it was on. I mean it was *on*. It was revenge time. I went looking for that Black man who had the nerve to laugh at me and imply that I wanted to be White. Right outside my building, I ran right smack into him. I stood, glowering at him, smug and victorious. He didn't say a word. He just turned and walked away. It wasn't quite the comeuppance I had hoped for, but at least he didn't laugh.

At first it felt like it was just Cicely and me wearing our hair in these short naturals. But then Mr. Tall, Black, and Nappy introduced me to others. They were "revolutionaries" who met once a week and talked about the rejection of European culture. When the conversation would turn to the platinum blond, beehive wigs that sisters were afraid to stop wearing, I would pat my Afro, feeling free. The mellow yellow Bed-Stuy beauty queen had been deposed, and a Black woman took her place.

ACT III: 1998

During my sixty-fifth year, when the sun was visiting Gemini, I made two related and irrevocable decisions. One was to retire from the job that I was holding at the time. The other was to redefine my image. I wanted to be an "elder," regal like the late, great Queen Mother Moore was.

I was already a mother and grandmother, a community advocate for poor Black children, a published writer, a craftswoman, a gardener, and a block captain. I just didn't have that wise persona. I decided that the first step toward achieving elder status was to turn my hair into a tiara of dredlocs.

Since the 1960s, when I freed my hair for the first time, I had vacillated between short, wash-and-wear naturals in the summer, relaxers for the holidays, and cornrows in between. But my locs would be the final emancipation. I would start them in tandem with retirement because I could not be afraid. I had to be in a position where I would not feel threatened. I had to consciously say to myself, "I am not trying to impress anyone."

This time, the image I was creating would be for me—not to titillate boys, to gain acceptance from girls, to be a beauty queen, or to prove I was "down." It would be an expression of who I was, or, more accurately, who I was becoming.

Now, there is this transitional place that lots of women call their "ugly phase" when they are letting go of the hair past, cleaning up their hair act, and getting ready for hair rebirth. Getting through the ugly phase was very difficult for me, but it was also hysterically funny. Beeswax in the hands of the uninitiated is a dangerous thing. My hair was soft, gray, and, in its own way, unmanageable. No matter how I twisted it, each strand did exactly what it wanted to do.

About nine months into the process, at my goddaughter's insistence, I did get some counseling. The loctitian shampooed, oiled, and dressed my crown. She also encouraged me to follow my heart and enjoy the freedom of my locs. I left her shop looking and feeling like a somebody. This marked the end of the ugly phase and the beginning of unanticipated benefits.

One such perk came from the young African American men I ran into at the University of Pennsylvania Hospital. As a part of my treatment for throat cancer—the result of decades of smoking—I went there almost daily, and the young brothers who worked there openly admired my hair and called me "Mother" or "Grandmother" instead of "Ma'am" or even "Miss Rosemary."

Sometimes I suspected they were giving me preferential treatment. Their tone of respect and admiration lifted my spirits and made me realize that I had achieved elder status. I was who I wanted to be.

My locs aren't perfect. The illness has kept me from giving them the kind of care that I would like to give. They are uneven, unruly. They don't have a style; they just are. But I love them anyhow. The radiation and chemotherapy did not take them out. They just hung in there with me, and I bless my head for that.

Rosemary Matthews (1935–2002) was a child advocate, award-winning activist, and published essayist. She died of throat cancer.

THE DARK DEN

Cynthia Berry

Photo by Rob Howard.

The dark tunnel of death where the afterbirth of a bloody childhood lay. The carcass of lost love, stolen intimacy, a life set astray. Tarnished and stained little princess awaiting the castle to be shattered and with it to be destroyed. Demon lurking at the door, taunting and displaying his toy.

I have hated my body since I can remember. As a little girl, my flat chest was treated as if it had breasts. I never had the luxury of yearning for a round behind, for it was slapped and patted way before it took shape. When I was too young to have a figure to speak of, my body was still good enough for uncles and older cousins, the grown men who invaded my home.

I learned to despise the area they called "cootie-cat" and "candy" the most. It was where I first learned fear. It was the place where I came alive in the eyes of my family, the reason for my earliest remembrance of being noticed. Always ignored by my mother and aunts, the men knew me by what was between my thighs.

The dark tunnel of death where the afterbirth of a bloody childhood lay. The carcass of lost love, stolen intimacy, a life set astray. Tarnished and stained little princess awaiting the castle to be shattered and with it to be destroyed.

As a little girl I believed my vagina to be a tunnel of darkness, a part that got too much attention. Before my sixth birthday I knew the pain of the penis. At eleven I knew I was cursed when a stillborn child lay in a toilet with a cord connecting me to it. This death would be wiped away through lies, but I thought my vagina was the secret. I named it Secret.

Holding childhood memories has destroyed its beauty. In adulthood, confusion has destroyed the possibility of my vagina existing as mine. I dread discussing sex because I can't relate to my vagina without feeling guilt, anguish, hatred, and pain. Questions have always caused me grief because my story differs so dramatically from others'. When asked, "When did you first have sex?" I always have two answers: at thirteen, when I made the choice to do it with the man who would become my first husband; and at six, when the decision was made for me.

Sometimes I wonder if in certain ways I am like a virgin. Although

I've had six children, I don't know if I've ever enjoyed sex. My vagina has never known an orgasm. It's as if it has never experienced first sex, for intercourse has always been in the power of someone besides me. With it I was to learn the euphoria of "love" that seemed to immediately transform itself into a lie.

The dark tunnel of death where the afterbirth of a bloody childhood lay. The carcass of lost love, stolen intimacy, a life slips away. Stained, tarnished little princess slain in a castle of snakes and wolves waiting a time to destroy.

My vagina has taught me there is nothing powerful in abuse, even though the abuser holds all the power. My damaged vagina turned me into the perfect whore, believing that in prostitution I would finally have a power over men. So when my first marriage ended when I was twenty-three—scarred by abuse that echoed my childhood—it became my hidden life. I knew no other way to define myself outside of what lay between my thighs.

Six beautiful children have planted flowers there for a time. But since their births, nothing of purity has grown. I look between my legs and fight against loathing. Now I have only the torture of padding the bloody spot once a month, douching it clean, and enjoying the pain of cramps and mood swings, its monthly demands connecting me in a way that reaches beyond the control of a man. As the pubic hair grows gray in spots and menopause draws near, I dread that I may retire its use without ever knowing it has life.

I fear that I will never fully pass into womanhood, the time when I will become whole, able to choose what happens to my body.

And so I write. From this prison in upstate New York, hundreds of miles from my South Carolina roots, I write. Ten years into a two-and-a-half-decade sentence for killing a man, a john, who became an unintended victim of my rage and depression and self-hatred, I have learned the power of my words. They help to make sense of the molestation, the rapes, and the domestic violence at the hands of two husbands. More than correctly spelled words and properly punctuated sentences, it is the only voice I have to tell what I have lived and what lives inside of me. Now, when I touch my vagina, I can still feel its past. But I no longer call it Secret. Today, through my words, I strive to write it into an existence without pain.

Cynthia Berry is a writer and peer counselor who is serving twenty-five years at Bedford Hills Correctional Facility. She appears in *What I Want My Words to Do to You*, a PBS documentary about a prisoners' writing group led by playwright Eve Ensler.

MY TUSH

Tracee Ellis Ross

B utt, ass, bum, booty, rump, onion, junk in the trunk, ba-dunck-ka-dunk, rear, and backside. These are some of the ways that I have heard other people describe what I just like to call my tush. All my life it has been getting attention. There was the time one summer when we were out at the pool and my little brother yelled, "Mom, Mom, come look at how big Tracee's butt is." My sister would always stick up for it, saying, "It's not that it's big; it's just that it's long like two bananas." I'd prefer to describe it as heavy and full.

I hated my tush when I was growing up and tried to get really skinny, fig-uring that would reduce it. So there were these two tests that I had to deter-mine if I needed more time in the gym or less food. First, the Grab Test. If I could grab my ass and still walk while holding onto it, then whatever I was holding was not needed and should go. Then there was the Jell-O-in-an-Earthquake Test. I would stand with my back to the mirror and look over my shoulder and stomp my foot. Too much jiggle meant I couldn't wear what I had on.

Really, though, there was nothing I could do. No matter how small I got, how much I worked out, my proportions stayed the same. Eventually I faced the inevitable—this was the body and the booty I was given, and I might as well start loving them. I've stopped wasting time trying to hide my tush. It's not like I wear clothes to accentuate it, but I have the type of ass that is pretty obvious no matter what.

I thank J. Lo and Beyoncé for proving to me what so many Black men have always known—that different body types are sexy. Being too skinny no longer makes me happy. Instead, I like my body when I have a body. I feel sexier and more womanly. I feel substantial.

Tracee Ellis Ross is the star of the popular UPN sitcom *Girlfriends*.

MISS PIGGY GETS DEPRESSED, TOO

Elon D. Johnson

Miss Piggy became my idol in 1982. There was just something about the way she tossed around her hair, lusted after the oft-evasive Kermit, and only bothered to learn one fabulous word of French: *moi*. Plus she was pink, which appealed to my inner princess.

When I was six, my mother used my reverence for the most famous pig on the planet to teach me one of her unspoken lessons. One day, during a standard post-school-day rundown, I mentioned that a classmate had called me fat. I *was* slightly chubby. But when that rotund blonde snatched one of my Crayolas and, upon my objection, spewed, "You're *fat*," I was appalled by his rudeness, not his words. *Fat* didn't mean much to me. *Fat* was like *ugly* or *stupid*, one of those disposable, generic insults that kids like to use.

While I told the *fat* part as nothing more than an addendum to a minor event, my mother repeatedly assured me that there was nothing wrong with me. Had my classmate said, "You're stupid," my mother would have casually retaliated with a "He's stupid" and never thought about it again. Instead, over the next two days, she dismantled the Holly Hobby décor in my bedroom. Down went the drapes and comforter bearing the skinny White girl in the navy blue hood. Up went the absolutely electrifying pink and gray Miss Piggy paraphernalia, which I didn't question because she was my girl. I'd be a grown woman before I would understand why my mother had evicted Holly.

I later learned that, as elated as I was to have Miss Piggy sharing my personal space, her marvelous life was not one I would live. Throughout her run on *The Muppets,* weight was never a problem. She was a star with a custom-made wardrobe and plenty of jewels, never craving male attention.

But if my mother could have peered into the future and seen her daughter at twenty-two—unemployed, fat, binge-eating, broke, and alone—she might have tempered the life of Miss Piggy with a reality check. She may have told me instead that when you become larger than the societal ideal, doors that were once held open are left swinging when you walk through, that the extra kindnesses from men dissipate, and that places of business fail to offer even the standard amount of cordiality.

Because when I no longer fit America's acceptable weight standard, the saucy, confident young woman who never thought about her size vanished into the thick and polluted air.

✳   ✳   ✳

Miss Piggy Gets Depressed, Too

I had a $140,000 Ivy League education. Had spent spring break reading French West Indian Literature, *en français,* under the Eiffel Tower for *fun.* I had my first job at a major music magazine. And a man. In short, I was feeling myself. Which is why I had no problem quitting when my boss's demands became more personal than professional. Dry-cleaning runs and Subway sandwich pick-ups were not a part of my grand plan.

So I was completely unprepared when the job market didn't stand up and take notice of my studies abroad and expensive diploma. Soon I was relying on my mother, stepfather, and boyfriend for financial support. I couldn't even pay my rent.

What I *could* do was eat myself numb. I consumed unspeakable amounts of whatever I could buy in the vicinity of my downtown Brooklyn studio apartment. French fries. Pizza. Macaroni and cheese. Fried whiting sandwiches shellacked with hot and tartar sauce. Food became a drug I'd use when I was feeling happy, sad, or somewhere in between. It was a reward. It was a sedative. Food was my companion.

At first I didn't realize how often I was gorging. I'd learned to overeat during my last year of college when I studied in Senegal. In a culture where waste is taboo and everything from fabric to foodstuffs is recycled, scraping every crumb off of a plate was expected. Back in the States, no matter how much food I piled on my plate, my social conscience would not allow me to leave one scrap intact.

As the pounds slowly surfaced on my back, chin, hips, and thighs, I'd go up one more clothing size. Chalking it up to haphazard sizing throughout the fashion industry. And then one day I happened to pass a full-length mirror as

I was taking off my shirt. In approximately four months I had gained forty-five pounds and gone from a size 8 to the outer limits of a 14. At 5'3" and 185 pounds, I was officially fat.

I started to hide. One evening one of my best friends begged me to go to some posh urban music industry event. I accepted the invite, but three blocks from my house an unwarranted advance to the tune of *"Hey Big Mama, can I go where you're going?"* led to my tearful retreat. I never even called my girlfriend to tell her I couldn't make it.

That night I dreamt that I was morbidly obese, and upon REM relief, actually believed it. I was 185 pounds but saw myself as over 300. The woman in the mirror was sloppy. Her skin folded over itself like melted Three Musketeers. She was a like a Salvador Dali painting; everything was floating around, but it wasn't the least bit artistic.

"Well, if you just did a few sit-ups and maybe lost some here and a little there, you'd be fine," my boyfriend of the time would say, poking my back where the regrettable rolls lived and pointing to my once-supple thighs. His touch felt like an electric cattle prod, so I'd order another serving of cheese fries to spite him. I was a table dancer: when my food arrived, I'd bless it with a shoulder shuffle. Then I'd eat, always using proper etiquette and at a normal pace, until I felt sick. I didn't care that it hurt afterward.

*   *   *

After nearly six months of searching, I got my dream job as a writer for MTV News. And the pounds just slid right off me. Yeah, right.

Working in the entertainment industry can turn some people (OK, me) into a mimic. I wanted the cutest clothes, best handbags, and fiercest shoes like the celebrities I was interviewing. I wasn't trying to compete per se, but I did want to prove that I could be just as fabulous on a budget. Instead of attempting to lose the weight, I went shopping at least three times a week. The smell and look of fresh clothes, no matter what size, masked my unhappiness while I continued to gorge myself.

In retrospect, I knew that binging on a daily basis constituted an eating disorder, but I refused to confront it. I was not equipped to deal with that level of reality. We Black women didn't have body image concerns. And even if we did, how could we trouble ourselves with something as frivolous as size when we had racism, AIDS, and a host of other battles to fight?

Moreover, the Black men I knew always chose an extra-thick woman over the girl who looked like she needed a sandwich. The way a Black man felt about a Black woman's body always reinforced that we didn't need to fuss over weight.

Admittedly, I did want to change the way I looked. The clothes I wanted did not fit, and the same men who had once flocked to my cinched waist and lithe legs now failed to see me at all. After a few months at MTV, I ran into a college friend who had always been overweight but had apparently lost half a person. Seeing her alone gave me the courage to ask for help. She told me about her weekly trips to a nutritionist and her weight-training workout at an all-female gym. Now that help had a face and a name, I was ready to seek it.

My major concerns, I explained to Dr. Davidson, were confidence, sex appeal, and health—in that order. What I didn't mention was my unnerving bond with food. I was too embarrassed. After more questions, he announced that he'd be running some tests and told me to come back in seven days.

Session two brought the truth. I told him that eating food made me feel good; how I would eat until the food was gone, even when my stomach was way past full; the way it took away any sadness; that it was also a reward for me; and most importantly, that I didn't feel like I had control. At the end of the hour he revealed a diagnosis, which was the last thing I had been expecting. I thought he was just going to tell me to eat properly.

The effortless way he scribbled the words on my file made my eyebrows scrunch up and my head tilt to the side as if this was some scam. Emotion-based eating disorder? Only narcissistic, insecure White women without real problems had those. "I'm Black. I can't have an eating disorder," I weakly protested. Unmoved, my Black nutritionist, who had doubtlessly dealt with other skeptics like me, explained that anorexia and bulimia weren't the only eating disorders, and that my unsafe relationship with food, forged sometime between college and adulthood, definitely qualified. As he talked about learning to eat effectively, I gave in. I silently bid good-bye to the McDonald's pit stops, where I'd refuel with a complete meal and something to go. I chose myself, dumping food as the dangerous lover whom I'd courted so enthusiastically.

I was washing dishes when I first felt the weight loss. I was scrubbing a glass when my hand, which previously did not fit inside the cylinder, slid right to the bottom. In time, I began shopping again; this time out of necessity. Retailers were at my beck and call, finding size 6s in every color. I became more outgoing in my workplace, and the positive feedback from friends, family, and men buoyed my confidence. Most importantly, I believed I had overcome my addiction to food.

Six years later it is still an everyday struggle to maintain a healthy relationship with what I put on my plate. I've gained and lost weight several times, eaten unhealthily, but never gorged again. I've admitted to myself that size still matters, that I rely on the excitement in a man's eyes when he likes what he sees. But while the happily-ever-afters of my girlhood didn't materialize in quite the ways I had hoped, my inner princess has somehow come out on top: she learned that outside her tower was a world that she could face and challenge and thrive in, one fabulous step at a time.

Elon D. Johnson contributes to a range of magazines and has held senior writing posts at MTV News and BET. She is currently working on her debut novel, *Reckless Abandonment*.

DR. FEELGOOD

Hilda Hutcherson, as told to Ayana Byrd and Akiba Solomon

Photo by Brennan Cavanaugh.

People always say that I do not look like the person that they expected. In our culture, the sexually confident, open and frank woman is stereotypically the slut or whore—a loose woman. Then they see me in a buttoned-up St. John suit and are confused—the appearance of the messenger does not quite fit the message.

I wasn't always this way, though. I grew up in a little town in Alabama in a very strict Southern Baptist family where sex was considered a sin. The messages I got about the sexual organs were for the most part negative. I was told not to touch myself down there and that this thing had an odor that was not good. I was supposed to be a virgin until I got married. And once I did, I was only to have sex when my husband wanted to. Oh, and marriage was supposed to transform me into a ho in the bedroom. But of course, after growing up with those messages, I was still a prude!

With this upbringing, you'd think that I'd be squeamish about training to be an OB/GYN. But that part didn't bother me because just as most doctors do, I was able to separate women's sexual organs from sex and sexuality. Throughout medical school and my entire residency we were learning to treat women's sexual organs, but we never talked about sex. Not once! We talked about pregnancy, but somehow we never talked about how women got pregnant. I suppose those babies magically appeared.

Soon after I started my practice, a patient asked me a question about anal sex. I was like, "Uh . . . well . . . *okay.*" I answered her question to the best of my ability using the medical knowledge that I had but I had no sexual knowledge. Nobody ever talked about anal sex when I was resident and I *definitely* didn't hear about it growing up. After that patient, I said to myself, "I really gotta learn more about this sex stuff!"

Before I got married, I saw my vagina as a gift that I was saving for a special man, which I did. I saved it and did everything I could to make him happy. For years, sex was all about him, not me. It was as if my vagina wasn't a part of me. But turning thirty was an awakening. After years of forgoing my own pleasure, something clicked. With age and the responsibilities of my career came a certain confidence and new concern about myself and my needs. I began to ask myself, *I spend so much time trying to please somebody else, making sure that he's happy, but what about me? When am I gonna get mine?*

So I decided to really look at my own body for the first time, to find out what gave me pleasure, and to feel good about being a sexual being. I decided that all of those negative messages that I'd internalized were bullshit. This period was about finding out what made me happy, and then having the self-confidence to say to my partner, "This is what *I* need. This is what *I* like." So that's why when I talk to my patients about sex, it's really from my own experience.

It took time to become comfortable with looking at my body. Like most women I had insecurities—I didn't look like the models in the magazines. I had received the message that good girls don't look, don't touch, don't even think about their genitals. I had to slowly progress through this self-discovery process. I looked at one part at a time and when I felt comfortable with that part, I went to the next. Eventually I was able to stand before a full-length mirror and say, "I like me"; I was able to take a mirror, look at my genitals, and marvel at the beauty of God's creation—so powerful, so perfect, so strong.

Hilda Hutcherson has been a practicing OB/GYN for more than twenty years. The assistant professor of obstetrics and gynecology at Columbia University writes popular sex columns for *Essence* and *Glamour* magazines and is the author of *Everything Your Mother Never Told You About S-E-X*.

NO FAIRY TALE

Norell Giancana

Photo by G. Giraldo.

"The good hair" is what it is, an open secret, something we all recognize without a textbook definition. Intuitively, we know what it means, what it looks like, and who has it—which is why writing about mine made me so uncomfortable. Nervous that putting my feelings and fears about my super-curly-when-wet hair in print might make "the good hair" real. And if that was the case, if I was going to put a name to the face of this "good stuff," then I could never stop defending all of us who aren't stuck up just because our hair lacks kink.

The Maureen Peals of the world have made it difficult for me. She was the snotty, rotten little bitch in Toni Morrison's *The Bluest Eye*. Maureen luxuriated in her "high yellow" skin and long hair, exploiting the adoration heaped on her by adults, calling other girls black and ugly when the going got tough. The real-life

Maureens have played up to all the worst stereotypes, making women like me, who were born with similar attributes, self-conscious about these features.

I have been the scared little girl begging for acceptance, feeling guilty about the attention I'd received for something as trivial as hair. At twenty-five, I still didn't want to own the uneasiness that I've masked with self-righteous smirks and running critique of all the music videos that exalt LSGH ("light-skin-good-hair") girls. I certainly didn't want to relive the time a friend shut me down with her own smirk and a question: "Norell, what do you think *you* look like?"

But after I put my tentative first thoughts into words and onto the page, I decided that it was time to put an end to all the fairy tales told about girls with "good hair" who have it made and get off so easy. So let me tell you about a girl with "good hair" that wasn't so good for her after all.

In La La Land, my hometown of Los Angeles, long-haired girls are a dime a dozen, and the hair you don't grow you simply buy. Growing up, my super-curly-when-wet hair that hung halfway down my back didn't make me feel special, but everyone—my mom, neighbors, family friends, classmates—always had something to say about it. My hair was sooo "long and pretty"; I was sooo lucky to have such a "good grade of hair"; I thought I was sooo cute and sooo much better than other people.

This last part—my supposed belief in my superiority—has always been the most painful. I *hated* the sixth-grade boys who told my best friend that her short, "nappy" hair wasn't as nice as mine, but in her envious glare, I could see that she hated *me*. I was always on the run from the slighted power of the bigger girls who threatened to beat me up to prove that my hair didn't make me special. I still smart from the back-handed compliments of female peers who congratulate me for actually being cool rather than stuck up.

So I did it. At twenty-one, during my last year of college in northern California's bohemian Bay Area, I cut off my hair. As six inches of the super-curly-when-wet hit the floor, so, too, did the preconceived notions and false assumptions that had literally swirled around my head. I was excited, empowered even. I had defied my mother's lifelong insistence on preserving the length and rid myself of this crutch.

Then I woke up.

The next morning, looking in the mirror at the crop of little curls, I couldn't believe what I had done. I cried at the sight of myself.

The day of the cut, I'd imagined myself as cute, but now I couldn't even stand to look at my face. This was the first time that I ever really saw myself—every feature, blemish, and flaw—without distraction. I felt ugly and exposed, like the Black female version of Samson, who lost his power after the duplicitous Delilah cut his hair.

Running my hands over my little 'fro, I remembered the times I'd laughed at friends whose trims had become full-fledged cuts in the hands of scissor-happy stylists. "Get over it," I told them. "It's just hair; it'll grow back."

I had missed the point. Sure, I had experienced bad haircuts and had to search for the right products, but it wasn't until I unwittingly stripped myself of my privilege that I saw how "good hair" had blinded me.

Unlike so many of my girlfriends, I had never placed scarves, shirts, and towels on my head to simulate long hair. I could reject the nonsense we'd all been taught about the inherent beauty of long, curly hair while still reaping the benefits. All my life I had been afraid to openly admit that I liked my hair, not because is was "good" or "better," but because I liked myself and it was a part of me. Now I wasn't so sure if I could like myself without that part. When I realized how vain and shallow my internal dialogue sounded, I cried even harder. Then, eyes puffy and nose running, I gave it up to vanity. I called my friend Amber, queen of the brown-skinned girls with killer confidence, to accompany me in my insanity to the fabric store where I was prepared to buy enough material to keep my head wrapped for eternity, if need be.

Eternity lasted only three weeks. During that time, I got used to my new hair and, strangely enough, my new, more honest self. I was ready to take a trip home. When I walked through the door, my mom acted as if she didn't recognize me. Then she looked appalled. Then she told me she hated what I'd done and couldn't make sense of why I would cut off all that long hair God had blessed me with.

I was surprised at the words coming from this woman who had told me about how my "crazy" father would comb her kinky hair while she was pregnant with me and say, "I hope the kid's hair doesn't turn out like yours." Apparently she had hoped for the same. Although my feelings were hurt, her anger showed me that I had taken a major step toward controlling my life and a leap away from letting others—even my mother—define me.

If my mother was disappointed, men were simply turned off. Gone were the days of being approached by a man even though he'd only seen me from the back. Apparently, regardless of texture, short hair wasn't such an attention-grabber.

With "long, good hair," I attracted Black men who wanted to know if I had Indian in my family and said ignorant shit like, "You must be mixed or Puerto Rican or something." Being a LSGH girl often held discovering that someone whom I really liked was attracted for only the most surface of reasons. I've lost track of how many times I have searched for patterns in a boyfriend's old relationships to see whether or not they all looked like me. Still, as much as I waged protests before, I was now stymied and insecure about the undeniable fact that I wasn't being found as attractive as before. A lot of attention may be wack, and from men I would never want, but I'd be lying to say I didn't care or had never made being noticed an objective.

As years passed and my hair settled back to mid-shoulder length, the conflict still persists within me. I've learned—fully in theory and haltingly in practice—not to devalue the way I look, but to interrogate the *thing* that makes my hair "good" or "better." Still, I am afraid to fully embrace my hair. Yet as I type these last words, I am satisfied, vindicated even, to have the chance to tell the other side of the story. I was once told that "nobody wants to hear your 'good hair' woes." But woes they are not. This is my story, no fairy tale, no happy ending. Just me.

Norell Giancana is a doctoral candidate in sociology at the University of Chicago. She is currently completing her dissertation on Black female sexuality in popular culture.

CALENDAR GIRL

Melyssa Ford
as told to Ayana Byrd
and Akiba Solomon

Photo by Ben Hadley.

Can't she do anything except take off her clothes?
She's just some chick who slept with a bunch of guys to get jobs.
Yo, isn't she that video ho?

I am the highest-paid video girl to date. I've endured all the snide comments and ignorant remarks from people who presume to know me because I'm on their television screens and in the pages of their magazines. But I'm not the promiscuous twit I'm often mistaken for. I am a businesswoman who has used videos to launch a multimedia career. My product is me.

Besides being the lead girl in hip-hop and R&B videos, I am a sex columnist for a men's magazine. I star in my own DVD. I've hosted television shows, and I've produced my own calendar, which I sell on the Internet. My job is to sell fantasy and perfection. When the cameras go on, I detach myself and play the sexy vixen who will turn a nigga out.

Of course, perception is not reality, and anyone watching videos should know that. No matter how the finished product looks, there's nothing glamorous about the process of shooting a video. In real life, it's three days of sitting around a set in the cold or heat, waiting to knock out your scenes and be done.

When I first started making videos, before I adopted the diva-but-professional attitude that I'm now known for, I had more to worry about than being too hot, cold, or bored.

I've had to deal with some pretty degrading situations. On this one video set, there was lots of Hennessy and weed. The video concept was based around a bachelor party, so it was lots of girls in their underwear being chased by guys. At one point I think things weren't going the way the artist wanted them to, so he started yelling at the crew, director, and the girls that weed and Hennessy had been provided for us to relax a little bit more. He was calling us bitches, saying, "Y'all better get the fuck open or get the fuck out!"

On that same set, I had to wear a very short, tight dress. I had some downtime, so I sat in one of the rooms where the food was set up. Soon one guy came in and then another. Within a few minutes, fifteen guys were surrounding me, and I was trapped. I felt like a specimen in a museum. I didn't want to get up because I knew if I did, they would start making a fuss over my ass. I kept thinking, *I'm sitting here with these guys ogling, trying to touch my leg and arm, trying to see what kind of girl I am, see if they can run a train on me.* I was so terrified of getting up. The dress was so short and my shoes were so high, I was afraid to even uncross my legs. Eventually a crew member came in and regulated the situation; he could see how terrified I was about even moving an inch. It all lasted about ten minutes.

Sexual harassment isn't the only thing that can take a toll. It's ironic: in a profession that uses women's bodies to help sell a particular artist and his music, all the girls wish they looked like someone else. Everyone wants to be Halle Berry or Britney Spears—voluptuous where you're supposed to be, nothing in places where you're not.

Don't get it twisted; I'm as self-conscious as the other girls. I'm from Toronto, miles away from the entertainment industry. Growing up, no one told me that the women I was looking at in magazines had been retouched, that people on television and in movies had spent hours in hair and makeup. I idolized Vanessa Williams, Vanity, and Apollonia. They were so beautiful to me, and I felt like I looked just the opposite. I'd been a chubby kid with a big Afro, eyebrows that grew to my hairline, and cheeks that looked like I was storing nuts for the winter. I had the body of a woman by age twelve. Throughout my teen years, all my friends were skinny, but I had the big butt, thick legs, 34D chest, 20-inch waist, and 38-inch hips. It was almost to the point of being suicidal, crying myself to sleep, miserable with what I looked like, hating to watch TV because of the standard of beauty that I didn't meet.

I've outgrown a great deal of that insecurity, but I can't say I'm immune to all the obsessions that women can have about how we look. Eight percent body fat, no cellulite, great abs, and perfect 34D breasts is my ideal. I can see my body's potential, but it's the legs, hips, and butt—the butt that made me famous—that I want to reduce. Men make a big deal about this butt, but I hate not being able to lie flat on my back because my ass is so high up that you can stick your hand through the huge gap. I always thought it would be great if I could shrink it, give the appearance of losing fifteen pounds.

Frankly, I'm shocked I didn't starve myself at some point, but I've never suffered from starvation disorders like anorexia or bulimia. Instead, for years, I abused thermogenics like ephedra and caffeine. I discovered the pills in my late teens. I was on my way to university and I started doing videos to supplement the money I was making at my two part-time jobs. I started because I saw ads of what this stuff did. Thermogenics are like uppers, giving you lots of energy. All you want to do is run, walk, do something. Sometimes I would sleep for two hours a night. After a point, my body built up an immunity to them, so I'd take eight to ten pills a day, chasing them with triple espressos. I quit thermogenics for two reasons. One, I was having dizzy spells, and spots would suddenly appear before my eyes. I was afraid that the drugs would kill me. And two, my boyfriend, whom I wanted to spend the rest of my life with, insisted that I stop.

Now I work out five or six days a week and contemplate every single thing that goes into my mouth. I'll pick up a cookie and think, *I should be eating fruit instead.* But I've learned to forgive myself and actually have treats every once in a while. I'd rather not focus so much on the physical and the superficial, but my body is my bread and butter right now and I have to do my job.

If I were to ever form a sustained, confident image of my body, one that isn't dependent on outside opinions, I would have to quit modeling and doing videos. It's just very, very hard to have a good and secure sense of self when you have to worry about the competition.

And then there's me. When it comes to how I look, I really am my own harshest critic. There's nothing anyone could say that I haven't already told myself. When I started out doing videos, the majority of the time I'd be the curviest woman on set. Because I didn't come from a background or a place where bodies like mine were celebrated, I was constantly surprised by and suspicious of the attention I would get. On my first big-budget video, for the Lox song "Tommy's Theme" from the *Belly* soundtrack, I was hearing stuff like, "I've never seen a body like yours before!" Everyone wanted to come in to the wardrobe trailer and look at me. Meanwhile, I was hiding behind a towel, thinking, *Do they actually like my body, or are all these flattering words their way of trying to get me to be more sexual on camera?*

That wasn't the only time I brought my insecurities onto the set. Even after I'd learned the little tricks to camouflage areas I didn't like, I was very self-conscious. In 2000, I did Mystikal's "Shake It Fast" video, which was based on the masquerade scene in *Eyes Wide Shut*. Because I have a mask, you can't see that I was crying my eyes out behind it. I hated my outfit, a halter top and short skirt opened up the side. I felt like I looked disgusting in it, really awful and large.

I became more assertive after "Shake It Fast." On subsequent sets, if an outfit was too skimpy or something made me uncomfortable I'd speak up. Once, on this 112 video, they wanted the camera to pan down my whole body and between my legs. I said, "Are you kidding me?" Although I felt unsure and a little timid at the time, the important thing is that I didn't let it happen. Now I have no problem controlling whatever I can. I'm in enough demand that I can ask to shoot my scenes on a closed set or to see the treatment in advance. Sometimes they say yes, other times they say no, but whatever the outcome, it sends a message that I'm the one in charge of my image and how I'm going to be depicted.

It used to be that I'd jump for joy when I'd get a call that such-and-such wanted me for his video. I'd be afraid to assert myself because I knew that there were other women who would be happy to do whatever they asked just to be there. But once you get kicked in the teeth, you either repeat the mistake or you learn from it. I learned.

For example, not once but twice *The Source* magazine ran photos of me where my butt shows but my face is cropped out. The one I was most upset about was for the cover. Another model and I are draped over Jermaine Dupri. I'm wearing a black bikini. My ass is right at his eye level. My face is covered by the banner, "Let's Talk About Sex!!!" No matter that we had spent two hours in hair and makeup. All that mattered was my profile—my tits, my ass, and my bare thigh. I felt so disrespected, like an object. I learned from that. And that's why I've become this machine, why managing my career and image became so important to me. Now for the average shoot, where I'm not making a penny past my one-time fee, I go in prepared to give about 50 percent. It has to be my own solo project to be worth a 100 percent effort.

Recently I stopped allowing photographers to shoot my butt unless it serves me financially or in terms of publicity. Every men's magazine wants the shot of the girl looking over her shoulder, with her ass right there on a platter.

I think it's too in-your-face, all sex and no sensuality. If I've got the cover of a magazine, I'll give you an ass shot. I also did a butt shot in my calendar, but I'm the one making the money from that.

I'm proud of what I've accomplished so far, but recently I've decided that I have a responsibility to myself to transition into being seen a different way. I've started to put on more clothes and try to only accept jobs that have a more sensual, as opposed to a racy, overtly sexual vibe. The fact that a woman who looks like me keeps showing up on magazine covers is justification enough for what I'm doing. What I do sends a message to full-figured Black women that we are a part of the beauty standard even though we're not rail-thin and White.

Melyssa Ford is an actress, television personality, and former video model.

BEFORE AND AFTER

Precious Jackson
as told to Ayana Byrd and Akiba Solomon

Photo courtesy of Precious Jackson.

Before I got diagnosed with HIV, I didn't really know who I was. I used to define myself based on whatever people thought about me. If somebody thought I was ugly, then that was who I was: ugly.

Early on, it was grandmother's voice I would hear in my head. My mother was addicted to drugs at the time and my father was runnin' the streets, so she had to raise me. Grandmama was no joke! She was old school, a strict Baptist, and she was trying to protect me from worldly stuff. That meant no friends at the house, no dating, no talking about boys, sex, or sexuality. Her thing was, "Keep your legs closed, keep your head in them books, and you don't need to know nothin' else."

She was serious about that not talking bit. I remember when I got my period at twelve. I was scared and I called out to her, "Oh my God, Grandmama,

I got my period." She came in the room and said, "Aw shit, girl, you know what to do," and walked right back out. God rest her soul.

Although we never talked about sex, Grandmama made one thing clear: If I got pregnant, she would put me out the house because she wasn't going to raise another child. To keep me out of trouble, she kept my body under wraps. At Washington High School in South L.A., girls were wearing tight straight-leg jeans with Gucci boots. But what did Precious have on? Long skirts, baggy tops, slips, and stockings, no matter how hot it was. I couldn't even show my toes! Even worse, from the time I was six years old, Grandmama made me wear girdles. She'd tell me, "Precious, you *know* your ass is just too big; you need to go put a girdle on."

I think my grandmother was so hard on me because she didn't want me to go through the same things she went through—having kids young and taking care of two boys by herself. But being raised in such a strict environment had a big effect on what I thought about myself. I always felt fat, ugly, and out of place. I didn't feel comfortable with my body, with the assets that God gave me.

I wear a size 16 now, but back then my body was *tight*. I was a thick size 8. I had big titties, like a D-cup, big hips and butt, and a small waistline. Guys at school would be like, "Damn, Precious, why won't you wear something tight and sexy?" They wanted to see what was under all those clothes.

As soon as I turned eighteen and went to college, I dropped the girdles and started wearing shorter skirts, tighter pants—nothing hoochie, but things that showed off my shape. Guys who never hollered when I had on my stockings and slips would be like, "Heeeyyyy!"

I took this in, and something clicked: *Wear tight clothes, get men.* I started believing the guys when they told me I had a body, and a beautiful one at that. I became sexually active and men became my gods. I would do whatever it took to please them. If a guy wanted to have sex with me, I would just do it. Most of the time, I just wanted to chop it up with them, to cuddle and share that intimacy. But I didn't know how to ask for what I wanted. I had been sheltered for so long and had really low self-esteem, so I just didn't know any better.

My mother, who was in recovery by this point, tried to tell me to slow down. She had prostituted herself when she was on drugs, and seeing how I was using my body scared her. She would say, "Focus on who you are. Find out what *you* want." She was trying to teach me that I was a beautiful person, that I deserved respect.

My father also tried to warn me. "Precious, you got a nice body, but men don't want no dumb women," he told me once. "Get to know a man. Be his friend before you drop your drawers." I was like, *Whatever, Daddy. I'm smart, but what these guys want is my body.*

Men know a desperate woman when they see one. I attracted a whole lot of verbally, mentally—and sexually—abusive ones. I remember this one guy who I really wanted to like me. I planned to have sex with him but wanted us to wait until his birthday. He wanted to do it much sooner. Me being the people-pleaser that I was, I got naked and got in bed with him. We could mess around, I told him, but I wasn't willing to have sex yet. He promised that he would just put the head in, but of course that was a lie.

In actuality, you would consider what he did rape. He raped me. But I didn't press any charges because, at the time, I thought, *I should have never been in the bed in the first place.* I was so afraid to rock the boat, that I believed I had given him what he actually took.

I met the man who gave me HIV when I was twenty-four. Today, I can do the math. He was a recovering crack-cocaine user. He had never shot dope. He had been in and out of prison. He was always verbally bashing gay people. He constantly begged me for anal sex. I don't know this for sure, but I think he got HIV from another man.

But back in 1996, when we were dating and working at the same customer service job, he seemed like someone I could trust with my body. We used condoms once, maybe twice, before he made it perfectly clear that he didn't like them. To be honest, neither did I. I thought they made sex less intimate. When he asked if we could stop using them, I figured that was his way of saying, "I'm your man."

Less than two years later, we're broken up, he's in the penitentiary for drug possession, and I'm reading his letter telling me to get tested because he just found out he's HIV-positive.

I froze. I hadn't even gotten tested, but I knew I was positive, too. My spirit knew. Two weeks later the results confirmed it.

I thought HIV was a death sentence. I was sad, but mostly angry and upset with myself because, once again, I had put myself in a bad position and now I was going to die for it.

My mother was my strength and hope. She understood what I was going through because she had Hepatitis C, which is similar in some ways to HIV. She kept telling me that I would live a long time, and she put me in touch with some HIV-positive women she knew. They came together and calmed me down.

In so many ways, HIV was a turning point. I got into mental health counseling to learn how to cope with the disease, but I ended up learning why I allowed myself to be used and abused the way I did. I say "allowed myself," 'cause can't nobody use you unless you let them.

I was empty. I had offered my body to these men thinking that one would come along and fill that void. I thought if I pleased him enough, a man would stay and complete me. But my mom and my daddy were right: There was a lot more of me to like than my body. If I lived with integrity and focused on what pleased Precious, I would complete myself.

A couple of years ago, a guy I was messing around with called me an HIV-infected bitch during an argument. Before I started going to therapy and rebuilding myself, I would have internalized that. This time I didn't; I broke it off with him. I was hurt by what he said, but I knew that HIV didn't define me; it was only part of who I was.

In situations like this, my belief in God keeps me strong, sane, and balanced. My spirituality is my number one priority. God got me through when Grandmama died and when my mom passed away in March 2004.

Every morning when I wake up I put on gospel music so I can get my shout on and praise God. I drink aloe vera juice, take my diabetes medicine and my multivitamin. In the evening, I'm at the gym, working out. Sometimes I get depressed, and get too tired and complacent to take care of my body. I don't eat right and exercise and I tend to beat up on myself.

To bounce back, I talk to myself, out loud if I have to. I say, "OK, Precious, you know it's been awhile since you worked out, and you know the aerobics teacher is gonna work the shit out of you. But you just gotta do it."

Ironically, being HIV-positive has given me a healthier sex life. I can't just do whatever with my body anymore. If I'm going to be with a man, it has to be because *I* want to. I see myself as more than a sexual object, and I expect more from a man than his hot body and a big dick. I need someone who can stimulate my mind first.

I tell guys up front that I'm HIV-positive. I told the man I'm with now the same night we met at a dance I went to with a friend. I saw him across the room, so I approached him and we started choppin' it up. He asked me what kind of work I did, and I told him that I was a treatment advocate for women who are HIV-positive. He said, "Oh, that must be hard to work with so many depressed women." I said, "I'm HIV-positive, and I'm not depressed." My boo was shocked a little bit, but after he did his research things were fine.

Even if my honesty had scared him off, it wouldn't have been a problem. Since I got diagnosed, I've become a connoisseur of masturbation.

Back when I was still dealing with all the wrong men, my dad told me to become my own best friend. I was like, "Oh, no, Daddy, that's nasty. I would never do something like that!" He said, "Girl, there ain't nothin' nasty about no masturbation. At least you know you ain't gonna catch nothin'."

Years later, when I was staying with my mother, I heard her say masturbation was OK. I thought to myself, *If my mother masturbates, it must be all right.* I tried it, and it's been on ever since! Masturbation is healthy; it relieves stress and tension and it tells you what pleases you. And sometimes I can get myself off so good, I don't need a man at all.

In terms of my physical health, I've been very blessed. For the past few years, my T-Cell count has been high enough and my viral load low enough for me take a strategic treatment interruption, which is basically a doctor-approved break from anti-HIV medications, which cause serious side effects over time.

When I was on the meds, the side effects were mild. I gained about twenty pounds—my breasts went up to a double D, I got some stomach rolls and a bigger ass, and my thighs started rubbing against each other. I also developed a smell in my vaginal area that wasn't there before because of the way my natural hormones interacted with the medication.

Believe me, it could have been worse. I could have suffered lipoatrophy, a loss of body fat in the extremities, or lipodystrohy, which causes lots of fat you can't burn off to collect in your stomach. I'm grateful that overall my body still looks the way it did before I got HIV. But more importantly, I honor my body because it's healthy. With a life-threatening illness, you don't have the luxury of giving up on yourself. You just keep on rolling.

Precious Jackson is a treatment advocate at Women Alive, a Los Angeles AIDS Service Organization.

BUMP, GRIND, TWIST, AND CELEBRATE

Iyanla Vanzant
as told to Ayana Byrd
and Akiba Solomon

I don't care what Black women's bodies represent to America. I only care what they represent to Black women. America has not included Black women in its ideal of what is beautiful. And when they do, it's a select few of us. There's Halle, Queen Latifah, perhaps Janet Jackson and Vivica. But you don't have Molly Jefferson down in Mississippi or Shaquana Gilbert in the projects. And today, with the collagen in the lips and the booty, that's not about Black women's bodies. It's all been decolorized, and we're meant to think that there is something even more beautiful in a White woman with large breasts, huge hips, and big lips.

So it's of absolutely no significance what America thinks of our bodies. The problem is getting Black women to recognize that fact.

That recognition is very difficult, though. Women of all races in this society are educated and programmed to please men. And men control the images that we see. A man had to create a bra. He had to create a girdle. He made those things that inspired him in terms of what is and what is not beautiful. Added to that, Black women have to remember that these men are mostly White, coming from a European perspective on what to idealize.

When I traveled to East Africa, West Africa, the South, all over the continent, I got an entirely new understanding of our bodies. Whether the body was large, the hips were broad, the body small or pregnant or old, women dressed according to their station in life. From the heavy country woman to the thin city woman, they dressed to suit whatever it was they were doing. I would go to the marketplace and see the Cash Madams, with the huge gelées and shawls and wraps around their waist. And it didn't matter what size she was; she wasn't in the mirror each morning considering liposuction. She was the Cash Madam, and this was how she was meant to look to run the market.

If Black women looked at our history, our culture as Africans, we would have another level of body image. The body beautiful that's placed before us in this country is going for something else. It's going for sex, for youth, and for seduction. We view our bodies as being for the pleasure of someone else, rather than the purpose of sustaining life.

The body is the temple of the spirit. Period. That is its purpose. And if a thing doesn't serve a purpose, if it is not doing what God created it to do, then it has no meaning. If an iron has no cord and no handle, then is it an iron? But what happens to Black women is that too often we get the image—to want to be fit, to want to be sexy and young—before we understand the purpose. So we constantly attempt to live up to the image, not fully integrating the purpose.

However, if you start from a place of understanding that the body is a channel for spirit, whatever you do for it is going to impact, improve, evolve, or somehow have an influence on your spirit. And then your body image, how you regard your physical form, has a purpose. It's not about being slim and lean so you can be a model. It's about eating right and healthy so you're a clear channel for spirit.

So we need to care for the body as the home of the spirit—feed it good food and give it exercise, lots of light, and sunshine. Touch it and talk to it; talk to your breasts, talk to your thighs, talk to your legs. If you have an agreement to be kind to it, it will be kind to you. You can tell when a woman is not caring for her body. It's not what she looks like that makes her feel bad, it's the lack of concern that negatively impacts her.

Like every woman, at least once a month, I look at my body and think, *I'm too fat, I've got cellulite, oh Jesus, help me.* My breasts laid down, bless their heart, when I was thirty-five, and try as I might, they won't get up again. I've pleaded, talked, begged, and spent lots of money on all kinds of wonderful bras, and nothing's changed. Sometimes I feel bad because I'll go into a store and what I want is only available in an 8 or 10 and I need a 12.

But I get over those moments very quickly. I know there are worse things going on in the world than my breasts hanging. My purpose in life as a teacher, wife, grandmother, sisterfriend, and facilitator of healing does not require me to wear a size 5. I've never had anybody say to me, "I can't read your book because your breasts are too big." Or, "I can't hear you because you've got a big butt and thin legs." All I have to do is remember my purpose and the body takes second place.

For me, the blessing was that I had no body image. None. Until I was thirty, my belief was that I was ugly and ugliness goes to the bone. I didn't even look at the body. When I decided to outlive my brother's teasing and taunting, I went from ugly to drop-dead gorgeous. Now I'm fifty-one and I still carry the idea that I am gorgeous. On bad days I just dress a little nicer and do whatever I need to do to heal my internal ugliness.

The good news for all of us is that once you hit a certain age, reach a certain level, and station in society, the body becomes secondary. I'd say anything over fifty. That's when the wisdom and experience, the clarity begins to show up in your face and in your being. Nobody looks at your body anymore. We love Maya Angelou. Have we ever said anything about Maya's body? I know she's not struttin' in no size 5, but how she drapes her body, how she carries her body is pure confidence. That's the way it should be when we're sixteen, when we have to do our manhunt and our man-keep and man-please.

But this desire to look visually appealing to attract someone is an instinctual rite of passage for the feminine heart. I've seen it in Africa and seen it in Trinidad. Which is why in my family we teach our girls—my goddaughters, granddaughters, all of them—the beauty, marvels, uses, and presentations of the body. We celebrate breasts when they show up with bra parties. We count pubic hairs as they arrive. Two of them have become young women, and they got mini-diamond earrings. They won't think they have to sleep with a man to get diamonds because they got some when they began menstruating. We applaud nakedness and dancing. We bump, grind, twist, and celebrate.

There are two things that women of any age should remember as they go through life. First, we must understand that God has made Chihuahuas *and*

St. Bernards. If you're a Chihuahua, good for you. If you're a St. Bernard, hallelujah. And that goes for every other thing in between—from a Poodle to a Great Dane.

And finally, the most beautiful thing about a woman is her heart and her mouth. Most of the people I've seen who are physically ugly, it is because their mouth and their heart are. So as a woman learns to open her heart and use her mouth to bring forth the messages of the heart, she will walk with a beauty that is unparalleled.

Iyanla Vanzant is a spiritual life coach, a best-selling author, a popular television personality, and the founder of Inner Visions Spiritual Life Maintenance Center and Bookstore.

INDEX

ABOUT THE EDITORS

Ayana Byrd is an author and journalist who divides her time between New York City and Barcelona, Spain. Her first book is the award-winning *Hair Story: Untangling the Roots of Black Hair in America*. A Barnard College graduate, her writing has appeared in numerous anthologies as well as magazines such as *Vibe, Essence,* and *Rolling Stone.*

Akiba Solomon is an award-winning journalist, columnist, and editor from West Philadelphia. A graduate of Howard University, the Brooklyn resident has been a senior editor for *The Source,* where she specialized in politics. Her work has also appeared in a range of publications, including *Vibe, XXL, POZ,* and *ColorLines,* She is currently *Essence* magazine's health editor.